"ORDER IS HEAVEN'S FIRST LAW"

Alexander Pope: <u>Essay</u> <u>on</u> <u>Man</u>

CONTENTS

PREFACE

Gold is where you find it! It is this law of our universe that has inspired thousands of people over the years to set out in search of riches. Only a microscopically tiny percentage of those seeking gold have ever struck it rich. Some have even lost what meager possessions they had before gold fever hit them. Alas, the consequence of chasing the pot of gold at the end of the rainbow has been, typically, overwhelming disappointment. And that's sad, truly sad.

Happily, there are other kinds of treasures we can pursue. These treasures reward us, not with things that gold can buy, but with the thrill of discovery. This thrill cannot be rated too highly. Suddenly discovering an interesting pattern or relationship in mathematics and conjecturing that perhaps no one since time began has ever known that fact, however trivial it might be, can have the same intellectual satisfaction as finding a vein of gold that no one else has ever seen.

The purpose of this book is to guide the reader into the endless wonderland of patterns underlying our number system. Once started, you may find that you want to dig deeper and on new and different ground, just to see what you can find. Such a quest can be exciting because the treasures to be found are infinite in number and variety. The amount of gold hoarded in vaults or lying underground still undiscovered is, after all, finite. One day the gold-seekers will have nothing to find, for all the earth's gold will have been found. But the search for patterns in the wonderland of mathematics can and will go on forever. There will always be something exciting yet to be discovered! You are invited to join the search.

"Angling may be said to be so like the mathematics
  that it can never be fully learnt."

Izaak Walton (1593-1683)

INTRODUCTION

EXPERIMENTS WITH PATTERNS IN MATHEMATICS has 55 experiments for you to perform. You will need a calculator in many of the experiments.

I hope that you will find in this book many new patterns and relationships. After performing each experiment, I further hope that you will ask "What happens if...?"

The question is a good one. It shows that you have a creative and inquiring mind. But asking the question is not enough; it is only the beginning. The true mark of a scholar is trying to find the answer to "What happens if...?" Thus you are encouraged, after performing each experiment, to ask and to answer questions I haven't asked, to pursue interesting questions and patterns in new and different directions, and to start investigations of your own. Frequently, nothing interesting will turn up, and your efforts will have been in vain; but sometimes a punch of a calculator key will suddenly reveal a pattern or a fact you had never known before. That's exciting.

You will find the answers to the experiments at the end of the book. I encourage you not to look at those answers until you have made a real try yourself. Use the answers only to confirm your results, not as a quick way to dispose of the problem at hand.

Finally, any pattern you may discover after working with the material in this book really should be shared. Show it to others. Better yet, send me a copy.

Boyd Henry
Dept. of Mathematics
The College of Idaho
2112 Cleveland Blvd.
Caldwell, Idaho 83605

EXPERIMENT GROUP 1

EXPERIMENTS WITH POLYGONAL NUMBERS AND ROOTS

Gratefully dedicated to Humpty Dumpty, without whose utterance before his fall, a dot would be just a dot, and that's all!

Most readers will readily recognize the square numbers. Here are the first 10 squares.

$$1 \quad 4 \quad 9 \quad 16 \quad 25 \quad 36 \quad 49 \quad 64 \quad 81 \quad 100$$

We call these numbers squares because each can be represented by a square array. For example, we say that the square of 2 is 4 because there is a total of 4 dots in the square; it measures 2 dots on each side. Likewise, the square of 3 is 9 and the square of 4 is 16.

```
                                           . . . .
                          . . .            . . . .
          . .             . . .            . . . .
          . .             . . .            . . . .
       2²=4             3²=9              4²=16
```

$2^2=4$ $3^2=9$ $4^2=16$

Let us agree that the square of 1 is 1 even though it is a bit difficult to argue that

.

is a square array.

In this section, you are going to investigate triangular numbers. As you might guess, triangular numbers are numbers that can be represented with a triangular array. Here are the first several triangular numbers.

```
                                                              .
                              .                    .     .
            .            .    .              .  .  .         .  .  .  .
       .            .    .              .  .  .  .       .  .  .  .
    T(1)=1      T(2)=3          T(3)=6              T(4)=10
```

$T(1)=1$ $T(2)=3$ $T(3)=6$ $T(4)=10$

In the triangular array on the right with 4 dots to a side, there is a total of 10 dots so the triangle of 4 is equal to 10. Likewise the triangle of 3 is 6, and the triangle of 2 is 3. We see that the triangle of 1 is 1. Our claim that a single dot now represents a triangle may not seem consistent with our prior claim that a single dot represents a square. To justify this apparent confusion of terms, we quote a precedent established by Humpty Dumpty.

> "When I use a word," Humpty Dumpty replied in a scornful tone, "it means just what I choose it to mean...neither more nor less."

> "The question is," said Alice, "whether you <u>can</u> make a word to mean so many things."

> "The question is," said Humpty, "which is to be master. That's all."

> Lewis Carroll: <u>Alice's</u> <u>Adventures</u> <u>in</u> <u>Wonderland</u>

Thus, when we are dealing with squares, the single dot . represents a square; when we are dealing with triangles the single dot . represents a triangle; when we later deal with pentagons, the single dot . will represent a pentagon. When we use a single dot,

.

to paraphrase Humpty Dumpty, it means just what we choose it to mean...neither more nor less.

In the triangle of 2, there is 1 dot on the top row and there are 2 dots in the lower row. Thus, there is a total of 3 dots in the triangle of 2. Look at the triangle of 3 and count the dots in each row. Starting at the top, there are 1 + 2 + 3 = 6 dots. The triangle of 4 is 1 + 2 + 3 + 4 = 10.

What is the triangle of 5?

```
         .
       .   .
     .   .   .
   .   .   .   .
 .   .   .   .   .
```

It is easy to see that the triangle of 5 is 1 + 2 + 3 + 4 + 5 = 15. Similarly, the triangle of 6 is 21 because the sum of the first six counting numbers is 1 + 2 + 3 + 4 + 5 + 6 = 21.

Alternatively, we might choose to display the triangular numbers as follows.

```
                                                              1
                                          1                2     3
                      1                2     3          4     5     6
1                  2     3          4     5     6       7     8     9    10
```

The advantage of using numbers is that we can tell at a glance the triangle of any given number displayed in this manner.

Throughout this book we will be making references to the trianglular numbers. We could, of course, write that the triangle of 6 is 21, but it is easier to use special notation to convey this fact. We will simply write

$$T(6) = 21$$

to mean that the triangle of 6 is 21. Similarly, T(7) = 28 means that the triangle of 7 is 28.

There must be an easier way to add the numbers from 1 to 100.

We know that the triangle of 6 is the sum of the first 6 counting numbers. Likewise the triangle of 100 is the sum of the first 100 counting numbers. It would be a lot of work to add all the numbers from 1 to 100 one number at a time. Therefore, it is very useful to have a formula to find the triangle of any number. Here it is.

$$T(n) = n(n + 1)/2$$

Thus, T(6) = (6 x 7)/2 = 42/2 = 21 and T(7) = (7 x 8)/2 = 56/2 = 28.

To find the triangle of 100, the formula tells us

$$T(100) = (100 \times 101)/2 = 5050.$$

That's much faster than adding the counting numbers from 1 to 100, one number at a time.

We will be coming upon the triangular numbers again and again in the experiments in this book, so it is important that you recognize them when you see them. We will also use the squares and cubes many times in our experiments. The table that follows lists the triangles, the squares, and the cubes of counting numbers from 1 to 25.

TRIANGLES, SQUARES, AND CUBES

n	T(n)	n^2	n^3
1	1	1	1
2	3	4	8
3	6	9	27
4	10	16	64
5	15	25	125
6	21	36	216
7	28	49	343
8	36	64	512
9	45	81	729
10	55	100	1000
11	66	121	1331
12	78	144	1728
13	91	169	2197
14	105	196	2744
15	120	225	3375
16	136	256	4096
17	153	289	4913
18	171	324	5832
19	190	361	6859
20	210	400	8000
21	231	441	9261
22	253	484	10648
23	276	529	12167
24	300	576	13824
25	325	625	15625

*****

1. Add T(7) to T(8); that is, add 28 + 36. The sum is 64. 64 is a square number.

2. Add T(8) + T(9). Is the sum a square?

3. Find the sum of T(16) + T(17). What is true of the sum?

4. What about the sum of T(24) plus T(25)?

5. Use the formula to find T(87) and T(88). Their sum is the square of what number?

6. Pick any two consecutive triangular numbers. Add them. Is their sum always a square?

7. Complete the formula: T(n) + T(n+1) = _____.

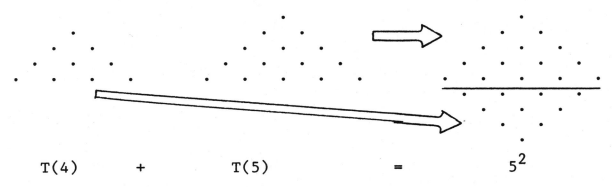

$$T(4) \qquad + \qquad T(5) \qquad = \qquad 5^2$$

Does this help you see why the sum of two consecutive triangles is a square?

*****

Experiment Number 2

1. If we multiply the triangle of 5 by 8 and add 1, we have

$$[T(5) \times 8] + 1 = [15 \times 8] + 1 = 121 = 11^2.$$

2. Multiply the triangle of 6 by 8 and add 1. Is the result a square number?

3. Multiply the triangle of 11 by 8 and add 1. Is the answer a square number?

4. Pick any triangular number, multiply it by 8 and add 1. Is the result always a square?

5. Try to complete the following formula.

$$8[T(n)] + 1 = \underline{}$$

*****

Experiment Number 3

1. We have already seen that the triangle of n is equal to the sum of the first n counting numbers. Now look at the sums of the first n odd numbers.

$$1 = 1 = 1^2$$
$$1 + 3 = 4 = 2^2$$
$$1 + 3 + 5 = 9 = 3^2$$

Fill in the blanks.

$$1 + 3 + 5 + 7 = \underline{}$$

$$1 + 3 + 5 + 7 + 9 = \underline{}$$

$$1 + 3 + 5 + 7 + 9 + 11 = \underline{}$$

2. What do you think is the sum of the first 10 odd numbers? Add them to confirm your conjecture.

3. What is the sum of the first 20 odd numbers? Of the first 100 odd numbers?

4. Write a formula for the sum of the first n odd numbers?

*****

Experiment Number 4

1. We select two consecutive triangular numbers, 3 and 6. Square each of these numbers and add.

$$3^2 + 6^2 = 9 + 36 = 45$$

What is true of the sum? If we check out the list of triangular numbers, we see that 45 is a triangle. It is the triangle of 9, and 9 is a square.

2. Next pick the consecutive triangular numbers 10 and 15. Square each of these numbers and add. What is their sum? Is the sum a triangular number? Is it the triangle of a square?

3. Pick any two consecutive triangular numbers. Square each and add. Is the sum always a triangular number? Is the sum the triangle of a square?

4. Can you complete the following equation?

$$[T(n)]^2 + [T(n+1)]^2 = \underline{}$$

*****

6

"This just scrambles my mind. The sum of the squares of
the triangles equals the triangle of a square!"

*****

Experiment Number 5

1. In the last experiment we selected consecutive triangular
numbers, squared each one, and added the results. This time,
instead of adding the results, suppose we subtract. What can we
say about the difference? Start with 6 and 3, two consecutive
triangular numbers.

$$6^2 - 3^2 = 36 - 9 = 27 = 3^3$$

The difference is 27, the cube of 3. Perhaps the fact that the
result is a cube is just a coincidence. Let's try another pair,
of consecutive triangles, say 15 and 10.

$$15^2 - 10^2 = 225 - 100 = 125 = 5^3$$

2. Another pair of consecutive triangles is 45 and 36. Is the
difference between their squares a cube?

3. Select any two consecutive triangular numbers; square each
one. Subtract the smaller from the larger. Is the difference
always a cube? Repeat this for several different choices of
consecutive triangular numbers.

4. Complete the following formula.

$$[T(n+1)]^2 - [T(n)]^2 = \underline{\hspace{2cm}}$$
*****

Experiment Number 6

1. In Experiment Number 1, we selected two consecutive whole
numbers and found the sum of their triangles. We discovered that
the sum is a square. In this experiment we first select two whole
numbers differing by 3 (instead of differing by 1). Find the
triangles of these two numbers and add. Suppose we pick 4 and 7;
these numbers differ by 3.

$$T(4) + T(7) = 10 + 28 = 38$$

7

What can we say about 38? It certainly isn't a square. Let's try two more numbers differing by 3.

$$T(5) + T(8) = 15 + 36 = 51$$

Another pair gives $T(6) + T(9) = 21 + 45 = 66$.

The three sums we have found thus far are 38, 51, and 66. None is a square number. But, what happens if we subtract 2 from each sum? The answers are 36, 49, and 64 and these numbers <u>are</u> squares!

2. Find the sum of the triangles of each of the following pairs of numbers; then subtract 2. (Note that each pair has a difference of 3.)

1 and 4	2 and 5	3 and 6
7 and 10	8 and 11	9 and 12

3. Pick other pairs of your own choice that differ by 3. Find the sum of the triangles and subtract 2. Is the result always a square?

4. Now pick pairs of numbers that differ by 5. Add their triangles; this time subtract 6 from the sum. Start with 2 and 7.

$$T(2) + T(7) - 6 = 3 + 28 - 6 = 25 = 5^2$$

Once again the result is a square. Is this just a coincidence?

5. Each of the following pairs of numbers differs by 5. Find the sum of the triangles of each number in each pair and subtract 6. What can you say about the results?

3 and 8	4 and 9	5 and 10
6 and 11	20 and 25	93 and 98

6. Pick your own pairs of numbers differing by 5 and try the experiment.

7. We may be about to discover a general pattern. What happens if we select two numbers differing by 7 and add their triangles? This time, we must subtract 12. Try this with these pairs.

1 and 8	2 and 9	3 and 10
4 and 11	19 and 26	37 and 44

8. Pick other pairs of numbers differing by 7; add their triangles and subtract 12. Is the result always a square?

9. Select two numbers that differ by 9. Add the triangles of these numbers; then subtract 20. What seems to be true about the results?

10. Let's try to find a pattern. The table below summarizes what we have discovered so far.

If two numbers differ by	From the sum of their triangles subtract	
1	0	The result is a square.
3	2	The result is a square.
5	6	The result is a square.
7	12	The result is a square.
9	20	The result is a square.

In the table above, the five numbers that are subtracted from the sum of the triangular numbers are

$$0 \quad 2 \quad 6 \quad 12 \quad 20.$$

Is there a pattern? It may be more apparent if each of these numbers is divided by 2?

$$0 \quad 1 \quad 3 \quad 6 \quad 10.$$

These are triangular numbers!

11. Now extend the preceding table.

If two numbers differ by	From the sum of their triangles subtract	
1	0	The result is a square.
3	2	The result is a square.
5	6	The result is a square.
7	12	The result is a square.
9	20	The result is a square.
11	___	Is the result a square?
13	___	Is the result a square?
15	___	Is the result a square?

*****

Experiment Number 7

1. Consider the following fractions. In each case the numerator is a square, and the denominator is the square of the next higher number.

1/4	4/9	9/16	16/25	25/49	49/64
64/81	81/100	100/121	121/144	144/169	

Can any of these fractions be reduced to lower terms? Pick any fraction with the numerator and denominator the <u>squares</u> of two consecutive whole numbers. Can any such fraction ever be reduced to lower terms?

2. Now consider fractions whose numerators and denominators are the <u>triangles</u> of consecutive whole numbers. (The first such fraction actually is 1/3, but it is not listed because it is the exception to what we are about to discover.)

3/6	6/10	10/15	15/21	21/28	28/36
36/45	45/55	55/66	66/78	78/91	91/105

Can any of these fractions be reduced to lower terms? Can all of them be reduced to lower terms?

3. Can we conclude that if the numerator and denominator of a fraction are two consecutive squares, the fraction can never be reduced to lower terms, but if the numerator and denominator are two consecutive triangles, the fraction can always be reduced to lower terms (unless the fraction is 1/3)?

4. When two fractions are to be added, we must first find a common denominator. Select two fractions to add using the following rules.

   a. For the first fraction, select any whole numbers you wish for the numerator and for the denominator.

   b. For the second fraction, select any whole number for the numerator. For the denominator, double the denominator of the first fraction. Then either add or subtract 1, whichever you please.

Example: If the first fraction is 5/3, then the denominator of the second fraction must be either 5 or 7. (The numerator may be anything. Let's choose 2.)

$$5/3 + 2/7 = 35/21 + 6/21 = 41/21$$

The lowest common denominator is 21, a triangle.

Select several other fractions using these rules. Is the lowest common denominator always a triangular number?

Experiment Number 8

In this experiment we have some odds and ends of computations for you to try.

1.   Pick any two consecutive squares. Add them, subtract 1, and divide by 4. What do you observe about the result?

2.   Pick any two consecutive squares. Multiply them, and divide by 4. What do you observe about the result?

3.   Pick any two consecutive cubes. Multiply them, and divide by 8. What do you observe about the result?

4.   Pick any two consecutive triangles. Multiply them, then multiply the product by 16 and add 1. Is the result a square?

*****

We can square numbers, of course, and we can perform the inverse operation called <u>square root</u>. If we can extract square roots, can we likewise extract <u>triangular roots</u>? Surely. Why not? Clearly, if the triangle of 6 is 21, then the triangular root of 21 is 6. Or we should say a triangular root is 6. After all, numbers ordinarily have two square roots. Do they also have two triangular roots?

If we can have square roots, why not also triangular roots?

Since $T(n) = n(n + 1)/2$,   it follows that to find the triangular roots of 21 we need only to solve the equation

$$n(n + 1)/2 = 21.$$

This simplifies to $n^2 + n = 42$,   or $n^2 + n - 42 = 0$, a quadratic equation. The equation factors, $(n - 6)(n + 7) = 0$; the solutions are n = 6 and n = -7. Just as 36 has two square roots, +6 and -6, likewise 21 has two triangular roots, +6 and -7. True, we cannot draw a triangle measuring -7 dots on a side, but neither can we draw a square measuring -6 dots on each side. Nevertheless, we accept -6 as a square root of 36 because it satisfies the equation $n^2 = 36$. Similarly, -7 is a triangular root of 21 because it satisfies the equation $n(n + 1)/2 = 21$.

Most numbers are not perfect squares, but we can find their square roots anyway. For example, the positive square root of 30 is approximately 5.477225, even though we can't show you a square with 5.477225 dots on each side. In a similar manner, we can "extract" the triangular root of 30.

$$n(n + 1)/2 = 30$$

$$n^2 + n - 60 = 30$$

Using the quadratic formula to solve this equation, we find that the solutions are n = 7.262087 and n = -8.262087.

*****

Experiment Number 9

In this experiment we investigate the nature of the triangular roots of any number, k. Remember, if n is the triangular root of k, then n must satisfy the equation

$$n(n + 1)/2 = k.$$

This simplifies to $n^2 + n - 2k = 0$, and the solutions are

$$n = (-1 + \sqrt{1 + 8k})/2 \quad \text{and} \quad (-1 - \sqrt{1 + 8k})/2.$$

Study these solutions and answer the following questions.

1. Does every positive number have two triangular roots?

2. What is the sum of the two triangular roots of any positive number?

3. What are the triangular roots of 0?

4. What are the triangular roots of 1?

5. What are the triangular roots of -1/8?

6. Do numbers less than -1/8 have real triangular roots?

7. Do those negative numbers that lie between -1/8 and 0 have real triangular roots?

*****

12

OTHER POLYGONAL NUMBERS

"It is a very sad thing that nowadays there is so
little useless information."
Oscar Wilde: Saturday Review (Nov. 17, 1894.)

We need not confine ourselves to triangular and square
arrays. We can create arrays in the shapes of pentagons,
hexagons, or any other polygon. The number of dots in such an
array is called a polygonal number, or a configurate number.

Here are some pentagonal arrays.

P(1) = 1   P(2) = 5   P(3) = 12   P(4) = 22

Notice that to expand from the pentagon of 2 to the pentagon
of 3, we start at the top of the array of the pentagon of 2 and
add additional dots around the perimeter of the array so that
there are 3 dots on each side. Similarly, to build the array for
the pentagon of 4, we begin at the top of the array of the
pentagon of 3 and then extend the sides to 4 dots each.

Here is the pentagon of 5.

Count the dots in the array. There are 35. Thus, the pentagon of
5 is 35. We write that more compactly as P(5) = 35.

Here is a summary of what we know so far.

n	1	2	3	4	5
P(n)	1	5	12	22	35

How can we find P(6), the pentagon of 6? Of course we could draw an array of dots and count them, but that would take quite a while. Perhaps we can find a pattern for the values of P(1) through P(5) from the table. Note the differences between the consectutive pentagonal numbers.

$$1 \quad\quad 5 \quad\quad 12 \quad\quad 22 \quad\quad 35$$

$$4 \quad\quad 7 \quad\quad 10 \quad\quad 13$$

The differences each increase by 3. We expect the next difference to be 16, and upon adding 16 to 35, we find that the pentagon of 6, P(6) is 51. Indeed, that is the case. Likewise, if we add 19 to 51, we see that the pentagon of 7 is 70.

The formula for the pentagon of any whole number n is

$$P(n) = (3n^2 - n)/2.$$

Thus, P(8) = (3 x 64 - 8)/2 = (192 - 8)/2 = 184/2 = 92.

There are hexagonal arrays, too. Here are the hexagons of the numbers from 1 to 4.

H(1) = 1   H(2) = 6   H(3) = 15   H(4) = 28

The formula for the hexagon of any whole number n is

$$H(n) = 2n^2 - n.$$

Thus, the hexagon of 5 is H(5) = (2 x 25) - 5 = 50 - 5 = 45, and the hexagon of 6 is H(6) = (2 x 36) - 6 = 72 - 6 = 66.

In a similar manner we can develop 7-sided polygons (heptagons), 8-sided polygons (octagons), or polygons of any number of sides we wish.

Here are the heptagons of the first three counting numbers.

We must pause here to discuss notation. We have said that we will refer to the triangle of 6, for example, as T(6). Likewise, the notation we have chosen for the pentagon of 6 is P(6), and we denote the hexagon of 6 as H(6). So far, so good. But what are we to do about the heptagon of 6? We have already used its initial letter, H, for hexagons. Our solution is to use the following notation [7-gon](6). Likewise the octogon of 6 can be denoted as [8-gon](6). This notation is not universally accepted, but we will use it anyway because it is fairly easy to understand. One of the weaknesses of this notation is that it is not very consistent. We will continue to use T(6) for the triangle of 6, rather than to use [3-gon](6). Moreover, there is the rather glaring inconsistncy regarding our notation for the square of 6. When we wish to refer to the square of 6, we will not use S(6), nor will we use [4-gon](6). Rather we shall use the commonly accepted notation

$$6^2.$$

Although this notation lacks consistency, we shall use it anyway.

"A foolish consistency is the hobgoblin of little minds."
Ralph Waldo Emerson: <u>Self Reliance</u>

Thanks, Ralph. We needed that!

From the drawings above, we see that [7-gon](1) = 1; [7-gon](2) = 7; and [7-gon](3) = 18.

Here are the octagons of the first 4 counting numbers.

[8-gon](1) = 1   [8-gon](2) = 8   [8-gon](3) = 21

15

[8-gon](4) = 40

The reader may wish to draw arrays for the nonagon, the decagon, or other polygonal values of numbers as we have done for the pentagons, hexagons, heptagons, and octagons of those numbers.

As one might expect, there are a variety of patterns to be discovered as we investigate the polygonal numbers. Begin by studying this table.

POLYGONAL NUMBERS

Number of Sides of Polygon

n	3	4	5	6	7	8	9	10	11	12
1	1	1	1	1	1	1	1	1	1	1
2	3	4	5	6	7	8	9	10	11	12
3	6	9	12	15	18	21	24	27	30	33
4	10	16	22	28	34	40	46	52	58	64
5	15	25	35	45	55	65	75	85	95	105
6	21	36	51	66	81	96	111	126	141	156
7	28	49	70	91	112	133	154	175	196	217
8	36	64	92	120	148	176	204	232	260	288
9	45	81	117	153	189	225	261	297	333	369
10	55	100	145	190	235	280	325	370	415	460

Here is how to use the table. To find the octogan of 6, for example, go to the column headed 8 (for the 8-sided octagon) and to the row headed 6. The entry in that row and column is 96; therefore [8-gon](6) = 96. Similarly, H(8) = 120.

Study the table for patterns. Some patterns are fairly obvious; others are elusive. For example, notice that every hexagonal number is also a triangular number. Look for differences between the entries of each row; of each column.

As you look for patterns it may be useful to know polygonal values of numbers not shown in the preceding table. Here are the formulas to find the polygons of any whole number.

Number of sides of polygon	Formula for the polygon of n
3	$(n^2 + n)/2$
4	n^2
5	$(3n^2 - n)/2$
6	$(2n^2 - n)$
7	$(5n^2 - 3n)/2$
8	$(3n^2 - 2n)$
9	$(7n^2 - 5n)/2$
10	$(4n^2 - 3n)$
11	$(9n^2 - 7n)/2$
12	$(5n^2 - 4n)$
k	$([k-2]n^2 - [k-4]n)/2$

*****

Experiment Number 10

1. In this investigation we are going to examine the differences between consecutive numbers in each row of the table of polygonal numbers. For example, the consecutive polygonal powers of 2 are shown below, along with their first differences.

```
    3   4   5   6   7   8   9   10  11  12
      1   1   1   1   1   1   1   1   1
```

Next we list the consecutive polygonal powers of 3, along with their first differences.

```
    6   9   12  15  18  21  24  27  30  33
      3   3   3   3   3   3   3   3   3
```

Now list the consecutive polygonal powers of 4 and find their first differences.

17

2.   What are the first differences of the consecutive polygonal powers of 5? Of 6? Of 7? Do you recognize the pattern of these first differences?

3.   If we had extended the table of polygonal numbers to n = 20, what would be the first differences between the consecutive polygonal powers of 20?

4.   For any number n, what is the difference between consecutive polygonal powers of n?

*****

Experiment Number 11

1.   Here are several sums for you to find. Notice that in each case there are 5 numbers to add.

$$1 + 2 + 3 + 4 + 5 = \underline{}$$

$$1 + 3 + 5 + 7 + 9 = \underline{}$$

$$1 + 4 + 7 + 10 + 13 = \underline{}$$

$$1 + 5 + 9 + 13 + 17 = \underline{}$$

$$1 + 6 + 11 + 16 + 21 = \underline{}$$

$$1 + 7 + 13 + 19 + 25 = \underline{}$$

Compare these sums to $T(5)$, 5^2, $P(5)$, $H(5)$, [7-gon](5), and [8-gon](5). What do you conclude?

2.   In question 1 above, the first sum was

$$1 + 2 + 3 + 4 + 5.$$

The difference between the addends is 1. In the second sum, $1 + 3 + 5 + 7 + 9$, the addends differ by 2. In the third sum, the difference between addends is 3, and so on.

Now, we ask you to find the sum of the first 6 counting numbers. That is, find the sum of

$$1 + 2 + 3 + 4 + 5 + 6.$$

Next, starting with 1, find the sum of the first 6 numbers with a common difference of 2.

$$1 + 3 + 5 + 7 + 9 + 11$$

Continue in this fashion. Next, start with 1 and find the sum of the first 6 numbers with a common difference of 3. That series will be

$$1 + 4 + 7 + 10 + 13 + 16.$$

Continue this process for several steps. What can you say about the sums of these series?

3.   If the series 1 + 4 + 7 + 10 + ... is continued until it has a total of 20 terms, what do you think its sum will be?

4.   What if the series 1 + 5 + 9 + 13 + ... is continued until it has a total of 50 terms? What do you think the sum will be?

5.   Consider any series with first term 1. If each following term of the series is greater by d (d a positive whole number), the first several terms of the series will be

$$1 + (1 + d) + (1 + 2d) + (1 + 3d) + \ldots .$$

What will be the sum of the first n terms of this series?

*****

It is just conceivable that we need not limit configurate numbers to regular polygons. With this restriction removed, the possibilities are endless.

Here, for example, is what might be called the irregular [(big bird)-gon](n).

To determine the number of which this is the [(big bird)-gon], it will be necessary to develop a procedure for extracting [(big bird)-gon] roots. This task is left as an exercise for students.
*****

19

Experiment Number 12

1.   In an earlier experiment we discovered that the sum of two consecutive triangles is a square. For example,

$$T(5) + T(6) = 15 + 21 = 36 = 6^2.$$

In general we can say that $T(n) + T(n+1) = (n+1)^2$.

2.   What is the sum of $2T(5) + T(6)$?   Compare your answer with $P(6)$, the pentagon of 6.

3.   Find the sum of $3T(5) + T(6)$.   Is the result a polygonal power of 6?   If so, which polygonal power?

4.   Is $2T(n) + T(n+1)$ always equal to the pentagon of $(n+1)$?

5.   What can we say about $3T(n) + T(n+1)$?

6.   What appears to be true about $4T(n) + T(n+1)$?

7.   In general, for any whole number k, what is the sum of

$$kT(n) + T(n+1) \ ?$$
*****

Experiment Number 13

In this experiment we call your attention to a variety of patterns among the polygonal numbers.

1. What is $H(5)$, the hexagon of 5?   Is the result also a triangular number?

2. Find $T(19)$ and $H(10)$.   What is true of these two numbers?

3.   Examine the column of hexagonal numbers in the table on page 16.   Is each hexagonal number also a triangular number?

4. Develop a formula that expresses $H(n)$ in terms of the triangular power of some number.

5. Find the difference between the pentagon of 6 and the square of 6.
$$P(6) - 6^2 = 51 - 36 = 15$$

Find the difference between the pentagons and the squares of other numbers. What is true about the differences in each case?

6. Next, find the difference between the hexagon of 6 and the pentagon of 6.
$$H(6) - P(6) = 66 - 51 = 15$$

What do you conclude about the difference between the hexagon and the pentagon of any number?

7. What is the difference between any two consecutive polygons of the same number? That is, what is true about

$$[(k+1)\text{-gon}](n) - [k\text{-gon}](n)?$$

8. If the square of a number is added to the octagon of the same number and the result divided by 2, what is true about the final answer?

9. Multiply any octagon by 3 and add 1. What is the nature of the result?

10. Add the triangle of any number to the pentagon of that same number and divide the sum by 2. What is true of the result?

11. What patterns can you discover among the polygonal powers of numbers?

*****

Nothing succeeds like success. Having pleased ourselves with such elegant discoveries among the triangular numbers, we reward ourselves with still more investigations.

The Reverend Henry Ward Beecher
Called a hen a most elegant creature.
     The hen, pleased with that,
     Laid two eggs in his hat,
And thus did the hen reward Beecher.

Oliver Wendell Holmes: An Eggstravagance

     Here for your reference is a table of the triangular numbers from 0 to 99.

	0	1	2	3	4	5	6	7	8	9
0	0	1	3	6	10	15	21	28	36	45
10	55	66	78	91	105	120	136	153	171	190
20	210	231	253	276	300	325	351	378	406	435
30	465	496	528	561	595	630	666	703	741	780
40	820	861	903	946	990	1035	1081	1128	1176	1225
50	1275	1326	1378	1431	1485	1540	1596	1653	1711	1770
60	1830	1891	1953	2016	2080	2145	2211	2278	2346	2415
70	2485	2556	2628	2701	2775	2850	2926	3003	3081	3160
80	3240	3321	3403	3486	3570	3655	3741	3828	3916	4005
90	4095	4186	4278	4371	4465	4560	4656	4753	4851	4950

To find the triangle of 57, for example, go to the row headed 50 and the column headed 7. There you see 1653, the triangle of 57.

*****

EXPERIMENT NUMBER 14

In this experiment we will investigate the sums of cubes of consecutive counting numbers.

1. Find the sum of each of the following.

(a) $1^3 =$

(b) $1^3 + 2^3 =$

(c) $1^3 + 2^3 + 3^3 =$

(d) $1^3 + 2^3 + 3^3 + 4^3 =$

(e) $1^3 + 2^3 + 3^3 + 4^3 + 5^3 =$

(f) Continue is this manner until you have the sums of the cubes of consecutive numbers from 1 to 10.

2. You might be surprised to discover that each sum in question 1 is a square. Find the square root of each sum. What can you say about the results?

3. Next we examine the sums of the cubes of the first several odd numbers. Find these sums.

(a) $1^3 =$

(b) $1^3 + 3^3 =$

(c) $1^3 + 3^3 + 5^3 =$

(d) $1^3 + 3^3 + 5^3 + 7^3 =$

(e) Continue in this manner until you have the sums of the cubes of consecutive odd numbers from 1 to 15.

4. Are the sums in question 3 squares? Are these sums triangular numbers?

5. Add the cubes of consecutive even numbers starting with 2. That is, find these sums.

$$2^3 + 4^3 \quad \text{and} \quad 2^3 + 4^3 + 6^3, \quad \text{etc.}$$

Divide each sum by 8. What do you observe?

*****

EXPERIMENT NUMBER 15

In this experiment we investigate the sums and differences of powers of two consecutive numbers.

1. First find the difference between the cubes of two consecutive numbers.

(a) $2^3 - 1^3 =$ (b) $3^3 - 2^3 =$

(c) $4^3 - 3^3 =$ (d) $5^3 - 4^3 =$

(e) Find the differences between the cubes of several other consecutive numbers.

2. From each difference in question 1, subtract 1 and then divide by 6. What is the nature of each result?

3. We now look at the sum of two consecutive cubes. You might find this pattern to be a bit elusive. Find these sums.

(a) $1^3 + 2^3 =$ (b) $2^3 + 3^3 =$

(c) $3^3 + 4^3 =$ (d) $4^3 + 5^3 =$

(e) Find several more sums of cubes of two consecutive numbers.

4. In question 3, you found the <u>sum</u> of $a^3 + b^3$. We now ask you to divide this sum by $a + b$, the two numbers we cubed in the first place. Then subtract 1, and finally divide the result by 2. What do you discover about the final answer?

5. Next we find the sum of two consecutive numbers raised to the fourth power.

(a) $1^4 + 2^4 =$ (b) $2^4 + 3^4 =$

(c) $3^4 + 4^4 =$ (d) $4^4 + 5^4 =$

(e) Continue in this manner for 5 or 6 more sums.

6. From each sum in question 5, subtract 1 and then divide by 16. What can you say about the answer?

7. This time we find the differences between fourth powers of consecutive integers. Compute each of the following.

(a) $2^4 - 1^4 =$ (b) $3^4 - 2^4 =$

(c) $4^4 - 3^4 =$ (d) $5^4 - 4^4 =$

(e) Find the differences between the fourth powers of consecutive numbers for several more pairs of numbers of your own choosing.

8. In each case in question 7 you found $a^4 - b^4$. Divide that difference by $a + b$, the sum of the two consecutive numbers originally chosen. Then subtract 1 and divide by 4. What is true about each answer?

*****

EXPERIMENT NUMBER 16

In this experiment you will investigate sums of powers and powers of sums.

1. Evaluate each of the following.

(a) $(1 + 2)^2 - (1^2 + 2^2) =$ (b) $(2 + 3)^2 - (2^2 + 3^2) =$

(c) $(3 + 4)^2 - (3^2 + 4^2) =$ (d) $(4 + 5)^2 - (4^2 + 5^2) =$

(e) Continue in this manner to find five or six more such differences.

2. Divide each result in question 1 by 4. What do you observe?

3. In this portion of the experiment we find the difference between the cube of the sum of two numbers and the sum of the cubes of those numbers. That is, if a and b are two consecutive numbers, we will evaluate

$$(a + b)^3 - (a^3 + b^3).$$

Evaluate this expression for (a) a = 1 and b = 2, (b) a = 2 and b = 3,   (c) a = 3 and b = 4,   (d) a = 4 and b = 5, and (e) five or six other pairs of consecutive numbers.

4. First divide each difference by $a + b$ and then divide by 6. What can you say about the final result in each case?

5. Our next investigation involves the sum

$$(a + b)^2 + (a^2 + b^2).$$

(a) Evaluate this expression for (a) a = 1 and b = 2, (b) a = 2 and b = 3,   (c) a = 3 and b = 4,   (d) a = 4 and b = 5, and (e) try several more choices of two consecutive numbers.

6. From each answer in question 5, subtract 2 and then divide by 12. What do you observe?

*****

If you find the triangle of a number and then square the result,

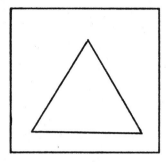

is that the same as if you square that number and then find the triangle of the result?

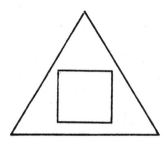

That is, does $[T(n)]^2 = T(n^2)$?

1.   It is clear that the cube of the square of a number is equal to the square of the cube of the same number. For example,

$$[4^2]^3 = 16^3 = 4096$$

and $$[4^3]^2 = 64^2 = 4096.$$

This is easy to prove because

$$(n^2)^3 = n^6 = (n^3)^2.$$

Now we ask if the square of the triangle of a number is equal to the triangle of the square of that number? If not, which is larger and what can we say about the difference between the results?

Suppose we pick n = 3. The triangle of 3 is 6, and 6^2 is 36. On the other hand, if we square 3 first, getting 9, and then find the triangle of 9, the result is 45. The difference between the two answers is 45 - 36 = 9. Let's see what can be discovered about all such differences.

25

Complete the blanks in the following table.

n	n^2	$T(n^2)$	$T(n)$	$[T(n)]^2$	$T(n^2) - [T(n)]^2$
1	1	1	1	1	0
2	4	10	3	9	1
3	9	45	6	36	9
4					
5					
6					
7					
8					
9					
10					

2. What is true about the entries in the final column? Are they square numbers? If so, what is true about their square roots?

3. Next we examine the sums and the differences of the cubes and the squares of a number.

First, complete the following table.

n	n^3	n^2	$n^3 + n^2$	$n^3 - n^2$
1	1	1	2	0
2	8	4	12	4
3	27	9	36	18
4				
5				
6				
7				
8				
9				
10				

4. Look at answers in the columns headed $(n^3 + n^2)$ and $(n^3 - n^2)$. First divide each answer by n and then divide by 2. What is true about the results?

5. In this portion of the experiment we look at the sums of the squares of the first several consecutive numbers with alternating signs. Find these sums.

(a) $1^2 =$

(b) $1^2 - 2^2 =$

(c) $1^2 - 2^2 + 3^2 =$

(d) $1^2 - 2^2 + 3^2 - 4^2 =$

(e) Continue in this fashion for several more steps. What can you say about each answer?

6. In Experiment 14 we examined one pattern of the sums of the cubes of the first several odd numbers. Here we discover a different pattern.

(a) $1^3 =$

(b) $1^3 + 3^3 =$

(c) $1^3 + 3^3 + 5^3 =$

(d) $1^3 + 3^3 + 5^3 + 7^3 =$

(e) Continue in this manner for several more sums. What is true of each of the sums?

7. Each sum in question 6 above is factorable, and one of the factors is a square. Factor each sum so that one of the factors is a square. What further pattern do you see?

8. The difference between the fourth power of a number and its square is quite interesting. Complete the following chart.

n	n^4	n^2	$n^4 - n^2$
1	1	1	0
2	16	4	12
3	81	9	72
4			
5			
6			
7			
8			
9			
10			

9. In question 8, divide each number in the final column by 4. You should be able to factor each quotient as the product of two consecutive triangular numbers. Try it!

*****

AFTER THE FALL IS OVER
THAT'S ALL!

*****

EXPERIMENT GROUP 2

PATTERNS IN THE ADDITION AND MULTIPLICATION TABLES AND IN THE TABLE OF SQUARES

Gratefully dedicated to Mock Turtle, without whose lack of appreciation of the three basic R's, we would not need to show you how interesting simple arithmetic can be.

"Reeling and Writhing, of course, to begin with," the Mock Turtle replied, "and the different branches of Arithmetic - Ambition, Distraction, Uglification, and Derision."
Lewis Carroll: <u>Alice's</u> <u>Adventures</u> <u>in</u> <u>Wonderland</u>

THE ADDITION TABLE

The ordinary addition table is familiar to all of us. However, most people don't realize that there are many patterns in the addition table just waiting to be discovered. Here is the table.

+	0	1	2	3	4	5	6	7	8	9
0	0	1	2	3	4	5	6	7	8	9
1	1	2	3	4	5	6	7	8	9	10
2	2	3	4	5	6	7	8	9	10	11
3	3	4	5	6	7	8	9	10	11	12
4	4	5	6	7	8	9	10	11	12	13
5	5	6	7	8	9	10	11	12	13	14
6	6	7	8	9	10	11	12	13	14	15
7	7	8	9	10	11	12	13	14	15	16
8	8	9	10	11	12	13	14	15	16	17
9	9	10	11	12	13	14	15	16	17	18

Now let's start looking for patterns.

Experiment Number 18

1.   Find the sum of the entries of the first row of the table.

+	0	1	2	3	4	5	6	7	8	9
0	0	1	2	3	4	5	6	7	8	9
1	1	2	3	4	5	6	7	8	9	10
2	2	3	4	5	6	7	8	9	10	11
3	3	4	5	6	7	8	9	10	11	12
4	4	5	6	7	8	9	10	11	12	13
5	5	6	7	8	9	10	11	12	13	14
6	6	7	8	9	10	11	12	13	14	15
7	7	8	9	10	11	12	13	14	15	16
8	8	9	10	11	12	13	14	15	16	17
9	9	10	11	12	13	14	15	16	17	18

2.   The entries in row 2 are 1, 2, 3, 4, 5, 6, 7, 8, 9, 10.
Find the sum of these ten numbers.

3.   The entries in row 3 are 2, 3, 4, 5, 6, 7, 8, 9, 10, 11. What
is the sum of these numbers?

4.   Find the sum of the entries in each of the other rows of the
table. What pattern do you see?

*****

Experiment Number 19

1. We now look at the diagonal sums indicated in the table below.

+	0	1	2	3	4	5	6	7	8	9
0	0	1	2	3	4	5	6	7	8	9
1	1	2	3	4	5	6	7	8	9	10
2	2	3	4	5	6	7	8	9	10	11
3	3	4	5	6	7	8	9	10	11	12
4	4	5	6	7	8	9	10	11	12	13
5	5	6	7	8	9	10	11	12	13	14
6	6	7	8	9	10	11	12	13	14	15
7	7	8	9	10	11	12	13	14	15	16
8	8	9	10	11	12	13	14	15	16	17
9	9	10	11	12	13	14	15	16	17	18

There is only one number in the upper right diagonal, 9. Its
"sum" is 9.

2.   In the diagonal next below, there are two numbers, 8 and 10.
Their sum is 18.

3.   What is the sum of the three numbers, 7 + 9 + 11, in the
third diagonal?

4. Find the sum of the numbers in each of the other diagonals indicated. List all of the diagonal sums. What pattern do you see in these sums?

5. We now look at the sums of the numbers on diagonals running in the opposite direction.

+	0	1	2	3	4	5	6	7	8	9
0	0	1	2	3	4	5	6	7	8	9
1	1	2	3	4	5	6	7	8	9	10
2	2	3	4	5	6	7	8	9	10	11
3	3	4	5	6	7	8	9	10	11	12
4	4	5	6	7	8	9	10	11	12	13
5	5	6	7	8	9	10	11	12	13	14
6	6	7	8	9	10	11	12	13	14	15
7	7	8	9	10	11	12	13	14	15	16
8	8	9	10	11	12	13	14	15	16	17
9	9	10	11	12	13	14	15	16	17	18

We are adding only those numbers in the body of the table, not those in the margins. There is only one number in the first diagonal on the left; it is 0; so its sum is 0.

6. There are two numbers in the next diagonal. Each is 1, so their sum is 2. The sum of the three numbers in the next diagonal to the right is 2 + 2 + 2 = 6. Find the sum of the numbers in each of the other diagonals indicated. Divide each sum by 2. What can you say about the results?
*****

Experiment Number 20

1. In this experiment we will be investigating the sums of blocks of four numbers in the addition table.

+	0	1	2	3	4	5	6	7	8	9
0	0	1	2	3	4	5	6	7	8	9
1	1	2	3	4	5	6	7	8	9	10
2	2	3	4	5	6	7	8	9	10	11
3	3	4	5	6	7	8	9	10	11	12
4	4	5	6	7	8	9	10	11	12	13
5	5	6	7	8	9	10	11	12	13	14
6	6	7	8	9	10	11	12	13	14	15
7	7	8	9	10	11	12	13	14	15	16
8	8	9	10	11	12	13	14	15	16	17
9	9	10	11	12	13	14	15	16	17	18

In the first enclosed block we see the four numbers

            2 3
            3 4.

Their sum is 2 + 3 + 3 + 4 = 12; and 12 = 3 x 4.

31

2. Another block of four is   6 7
                                 7 8.

What is the sum of these four numbers?   Can this sum be factored so that one of the factors is 4?   If so, what is the other factor?

3. Add the four numbers in the block   12 13
                                        13 14.

Is this sum factorable? Is 4 a factor? What is the other factor?

4. Find the sums of the four numbers in the other blocks indicated. Make up some of your own. Can you predict in advance what the sums will be?

5. What is the rule for quickly finding the sum without actually adding the four numbers?

*****

Experiment Number 21

1. We now look at the sums of blocks of nine numbers.

+	0	1	2	3	4	5	6	7	8	9
0	0	1	2	3	4	5	6	7	8	9
1	1	2	3	4	5	6	7	8	9	10
2	2	3	4	5	6	7	8	9	10	11
3	3	4	5	6	7	8	9	10	11	12
4	4	5	6	7	8	9	10	11	12	13
5	5	6	7	8	9	10	11	12	13	14
6	6	7	8	9	10	11	12	13	14	15
7	7	8	9	10	11	12	13	14	15	16
8	8	9	10	11	12	13	14	15	16	17
9	9	10	11	12	13	14	15	16	17	18

What is the sum of the nine numbers in the block   2 3 4
                                                    3 4 5
                                                    4 5 6 ?

Can this sum be factored?   Is one of the factors 9?   If so, what is the other factor?

2. Find the sum of the nine numbers in the block   6 7 8
                                                   7 8 9
                                                   8 9 10.

What is true of this sum?

3.   Find the sum of the numbers in the other indicated block of nine numbers. Select several blocks of nine of your own choosing. Can you predict the sum without actually adding all nine numbers?

4.   What is the rule for finding the sum of the nine numbers in any square block?

5.   Next pick sixteen numbers in a block, such as

```
6  7  8  9
7  8  9 10
8  9 10 11
9 10 11 12.
```

What is the sum of these sixteen numbers. Does 16 divide the sum? If so, what is the other factor?

6.   State a rule for finding the sum of the numbers in a block of sixteen numbers.

7.   The numbers in the body of the entire addition table constitute a block of 100 numbers. What do you think is the sum of all 100 numbers in the table?

*****

Experiment Number 22

1.   In this experiment we will investigate the sum of the numbers in several other configurations in the addition table.

```
+ | 0  1  2  3  4  5  6  7  8  9
--+----------------------------
0 | 0  1  2  3  4  5  6  7  8  9
1 | 1  2  3  4  5  6  7  8  9 10
2 | 2  3  4  5  6  7  8  9 10 11
3 | 3  4  5  6  7  8  9 10 11 12
4 | 4  5  6  7  8  9 10 11 12 13
5 | 5  6  7  8  9 10 11 12 13 14
6 | 6  7  8  9 10 11 12 13 14 15
7 | 7  8  9 10 11 12 13 14 15 16
8 | 8  9 10 11 12 13 14 15 16 17
9 | 9 10 11 12 13 14 15 16 17 18
```

2. What is the sum of the five numbers in the cross

$$
\begin{array}{ccc}
 & 3 & \\
3 & 4 & 5 \\
 & 5 & \quad ?
\end{array}
$$

3. Find the sums of the five numbers in each of the other crosses indicated.

4.   Choose several other crosses of five numbers and find the sums. What can you say about those sums?

5.   There are seven numbers in an H-shaped configuration in the table above. What is the sum of the numbers in that H?

6.   Pick several H-shaped configurations of your own choosing. What is true of the sum of the seven numbers in any such H?

33

"You picked 'H' to find a pattern," complained Mock
   Turtle, "and 'H' is for Hare! How about us Turtles?
   We count, too, you know. Why not pick 'T' for
   Turtle?"
   B. Henry: with apologies to Lewis Carroll

"We count too!"

7. Why not, indeed? Below are several T-shaped configurations
taken from the addition table.

```
3  4  5        4  5  6        8  9 10       13 14 15
   5              6              10             15
   6              7              11             16
```

Find the sums of the five numbers in each T.

8. Can you discover a rule for their sums? It is not as simple as
the rules for the sums of numbers in squares, crosses, and H's.

9. Suppose that Mock Turtle and March Hare decided to team up and
investigate the sum of the numbers in an 'M' (for both Mock and
March) and decided to select their M's in this manner.

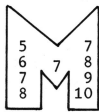

Can you find a formula for the sum of the nine numbers in any
such M?

10. Make up other configurations of your own. Try to discover a
formula for the sums of the numbers in each of your
configurations.

*****

34

1. In this experiment we will look for patterns between products of pairs of numbers selected from the addition table.

```
+ | 0  1  2  3  4  5  6  7  8  9
--+-----------------------------
0 | 0  1  2  3  4  5  6  7  8  9
1 | 1  2  3  4  5  6  7  8  9 10
2 | 2  3  4  5  6  7  8  9 10 11
3 | 3  4  5  6  7  8  9 10 11 12
4 | 4  5  6  7  8  9 10 11 12 13
5 | 5  6  7  8  9 10 11 12 13 14
6 | 6  7  8  9 10 11 12 13 14 15
7 | 7  8  9 10 11 12 13 14 15 16
8 | 8  9 10 11 12 13 14 15 16 17
9 | 9 10 11 12 13 14 15 16 17 18
```

In the table you see several X-shaped configurations. We will find the product of the two numbers at the end of one of the cross bars of the X, and subtract that product from the product of the two numbers on the ends of the other cross bar. For example, on this X

the products are 4 x 4 = 16 and 2 x 6 = 12. The difference between these two products is 4. To simplify our terminology we shall refer to these products as the cross products.

2. Find the cross products of this X.

What is the difference between the two cross products?

3. Find the differences between the two cross products on each of the other X's indicated on the table above. What are the differences between those cross products?

4. Select any 3 by 3 block of numbers from the table that you wish. Draw an X such as we have done. What is the difference between the two cross products?

5. Now, we change the rules. Instead of subtracting one cross product from the other, go back and multiply the two cross products. In our example in question 1 the two cross products are 16 and 12; their product is 192. Maybe you can't say anything special about 192, but if you add 4, the result is 196, and 196 is the square of 14.

6.   Multiply the cross products found in question 2 and then add 4. What is the result? Is it a square? If so, the square of what number?

7.   Multiply the cross products of each of the other X's indicated in the addition table. Add 4. Is the result a square? Pick X's of your own choosing; multiply the cross products and add 4. Is the result always a square?

8.   State a formula that will predict the result when the product of the two cross products is increased by 4.

*****

Experiment Number 24

1. This experiment is similar to the first part of Experiment Number 23, but this time we will be looking at the differences between the cross products of larger X's.

```
+ | 0  1  2  3  4  5  6  7  8  9
--+------------------------------
0 | 0  1  2  3  4  5  6  7  8  9
1 | 1 (2) 3  4 (5) 6  7  8  9 10
2 | 2  3  4  5  6 (7) 8  9 (10) 11
3 | 3  4  5  6  7  8  9 10 11 12
4 | 4 (5) 6  7 (8) 9 10 11 12 13
5 | 5  6  7  8  9 (10) 11 12 (13) 14
6 |(6) 7  8 (9) 10 11 (12) 13 14 (15)
7 | 7  8  9 10 11 12 13 14 15 16
8 | 8  9 10 11 12 13 14 15 16 17
9 |(9) 10 11 (12) 13 14 (15) 16 17 (18)
```

The tips of the X's in this array are at the corners of a 4 by 4 block of numbers. Find the differences between the cross products in each of the indicated X's.

2.   Select some X's this size of your own choosing. What are the differences between their cross products?

3.   Pick an X that is even larger. For example, what is the difference between the two cross products of the X shown below?

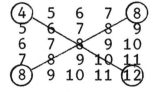

4. If we start with an n by n array of numbers, what is the difference between the cross products of the tips of the X?

*****

36

1. Select the four corner numbers of the addition table.

+	0	1	2	3	4	5	6	7	8	9
0	0	1	2	3	4	5	6	7	8	9
1	1	2	3	4	5	6	7	8	9	10
2	2	3	4	5	6	7	8	9	10	11
3	3	4	5	6	7	8	9	10	11	12
4	4	5	6	7	8	9	10	11	12	13
5	5	6	7	8	9	10	11	12	13	14
6	6	7	8	9	10	11	12	13	14	15
7	7	8	9	10	11	12	13	14	15	16
8	8	9	10	11	12	13	14	15	16	17
9	9	10	11	12	13	14	15	16	17	18

Those four corner numbers are 0, 9, 9, and 18. What is their sum? What can we say about that sum?

2. Next find the sum of all 16 numbers in the four 2 by 2 blocks in the four corners of the table.

+	0	1	2	3	4	5	6	7	8	9
0	0	1	2	3	4	5	6	7	8	9
1	1	2	3	4	5	6	7	8	9	10
2	2	3	4	5	6	7	8	9	10	11
3	3	4	5	6	7	8	9	10	11	12
4	4	5	6	7	8	9	10	11	12	13
5	5	6	7	8	9	10	11	12	13	14
6	6	7	8	9	10	11	12	13	14	15
7	7	8	9	10	11	12	13	14	15	16
8	8	9	10	11	12	13	14	15	16	17
9	9	10	11	12	13	14	15	16	17	18

What is the sum of these 16 numbers? Is it a square?

3. Next find the sum of all 36 numbers in the four 3 by 3 corner blocks. Is the sum a square?

```
0  1  2          7  8  9
1  2  3          8  9 10
2  3  4          9 10 11


7  8  9         14 15 16
8  9 10         15 16 17
9 10 11         16 17 18
```

4. Continue this experiment. Find the sum of all the numbers in the four corner blocks measuring 4 by 4. Can you predict what the sum will be before you actually add all these numbers?

5. The entire addition table is used if each of the four corner blocks measures 5 by 5. What do you think is the sum of all 100 numbers in these four blocks (and therefore the sum of all the numbers in the table)?

*****

PATTERNS IN THE MULTIPLICATION TABLE

Gratefully dedicated to Walrus, without whose problem with maids and brooms, the multiplication table might never have been needed at all.

The Walrus and the Carpenter
  Were walking close at hand:
They wept like anything to see
  Such quantities of sand:
"If this were only cleared away,"
  They said, "It would be grand!"

"If seven maids with seven mops
  Swept it for half a year,
Do you suppose," the Walrus said
  "That they could get it clear?"
"I doubt it," said the carpenter,
  And shed a bitter tear.

Lewis Carroll: Through the Looking Glass

Since the addition table has so many interesting patterns hiding within it, one might well ask about the multiplication table.   Is it, too, full of surprises? Here it is. Before going on, see what you can find.

x	1	2	3	4	5	6	7	8	9
1	1	2	3	4	5	6	7	8	9
2	2	4	6	8	10	12	14	16	18
3	3	6	9	12	15	18	21	24	27
4	4	8	12	16	20	24	28	32	36
5	5	10	15	20	25	30	35	40	45
6	6	12	18	24	30	36	42	48	54
7	7	14	21	28	35	42	49	56	63
8	8	16	24	32	40	48	56	64	72
9	9	18	27	36	45	54	63	72	81

*****

1.   In Experiment 19 you are asked to explore the diagonal sums. We do the same thing here.

x	1	2	3	4	5	6	7	8	9
1	1	2	3	4	5	6	7	8	9
2	2	4	6	8	10	12	14	16	18
3	3	6	9	12	15	18	21	24	27
4	4	8	12	16	20	24	28	32	36
5	5	10	15	20	25	30	35	40	45
6	6	12	18	24	30	36	42	48	54
7	7	14	21	28	35	42	49	56	63
8	8	16	24	32	40	48	56	64	72
9	9	18	27	36	45	54	63	72	81

There is only one number in the upper diagonal; it is 9. Thus, its sum is 9.

2.   In the next diagonal there are two numbers, 8 and 18. Their sum, of course, is 26. What is the sum of the three numbers in the diagonal below that, that is, 7 + 16 + 27?

3.   Find each of the other diagonal sums.   At first glance, and even at second glance, these sums don't appear to be particularly promising. Let's take a closer look.

4.   The sum of the top diagonal is 9. Multiply it by 3/27. The second diagonal sum is 26; multiply it by 3/26. Multiply the third diagonal sum by 3/25; the fourth diagonal sum by 3/24; the next by 3/23. Continue in this manner, each time multiplying by a fraction in which the denominator decreases by 1; and the numerator is 3. What do you observe?

*****

In this experiment we investigate the sums of the numbers on the diagonals running from the upper right to lower left.

x	1	2	3	4	5	6	7	8	9
1	1	2	3	4	5	6	7	8	9
2	2	4	6	8	10	12	14	16	18
3	3	6	9	12	15	18	21	24	27
4	4	8	12	16	20	24	28	32	36
5	5	10	15	20	25	30	35	40	45
6	6	12	18	24	30	36	42	48	54
7	7	14	21	28	35	42	49	56	63
8	8	16	24	32	40	48	56	64	72
9	9	18	27	36	45	54	63	72	81

1. The only number in the top diagonal is 1; so the sum is 1. The sum of 2 + 2 in the 2nd diagonal is 4. Find the sum of the numbers in each of the other indicated diagonals.

2. As in Experiment 26, the pattern of these sums is not immediately obvious. Multiply the first sum, 1, by 3/3; multiply the next sum by 3/4; the next by 3/5; and the next by 3/6. Continue in this manner. Each time increase the denominator of the multiplier by 1. What can you say about the results?

3. Once again write the sums of the numbers in each of the diagonals indicated. This time, multiply each sum by 6. Each such product should be refactorable into 3 consecutive counting numbers. For example, the first sum is 1 and

$$1 \times 6 = 6 = 1 \times 2 \times 3.$$

The second diagonal sum is 4 and

$$4 \times 6 = 24 = 2 \times 3 \times 4.$$

Multiply each of the other diagonal sums by 6. Can that product always be factored into the product of three consecutive numbers?

*****

Experiment Number 28

1. Select any two rows of the multiplication table and write one row directly under the other. For example, if we select row 2 and row 5 we have

x									
2	2	4	6	8	10	12	14	16	18
5	5	10	15	20	25	30	35	40	45 .

2. Treat the pairs of numbers one over the other as fractions. That is, treat

$$\frac{2}{5} \quad \text{and} \quad \frac{4}{10}$$

as if they were the fractions 2/5 and 4/10. Treat each of the other pairs as fractions also. What can you say about the value of all of these fractions?

3. Expain how a person could use the multiplication table to reduce fractions such as 12/30 or 32/56 to lowest terms.

*****

x	1	2	3	4	5	6	7	8	9
1	1	2	3	4	5	6	7	8	9
2	2	4	6	8	10	12	14	16	18
3	3	6	9	12	15	18	21	24	27
4	4	8	12	16	20	24	28	32	36
5	5	10	15	20	25	30	35	40	45
6	6	12	18	24	30	36	42	48	54
7	7	14	21	28	35	42	49	56	63
8	8	16	24	32	40	48	56	64	72
9	9	18	27	36	45	54	63	72	81

1. This multiplication table has been overlayed by several rectangles. The numbers at the vertices of one of the rectangles are 2, 6, 3, and 9. Find the product of these four numbers. Is that product a square?

2. The vertices of another rectangle are 14, 35, 18, and 45. Find their product. Is it a square?

3. Find the products of the four numbers at the vertices of each of the other rectangles indicated. Is the product always a square?

4. Select any rectangle from the multiplication table that you wish. What is always true of the product of the four vertex numbers? State the rule to predict the product.

5. In the next portion of this experiment we will add the four numbers at the vertices, instead of multiplying them. The vertices of the rectangle in step 1 are 2, 6, 3, and 9. Their sum is 20. One way to factor 20 is

$$20 = 4 \times 5.$$

There is a relationship between these factors and the numbers in the vertices? This relationship may not be immediately obvious so you may need to investigate several different rectangles before you are ready to make a decision.

For example, the numbers at vertices of another rectangle are 14, 35, 18 and 45. The sum of these four numbers is 112, and

$$112 = 7 \times 16.$$

Experiment with the sum of the numbers at the vertices of other rectangles. The sum is always factorable. Can you spot the pattern for the two factors of each sum?

*****

In this experiment we have overlaid the multiplication table with octagons.

```
x │  1   2   3   4   5   6   7   8   9
──┼────────────────────────────────────
1 │  1   2   3   4   5   6   7   8   9
2 │  2   4   6   8  10  12  14  16  18
3 │  3   6   9  12  15  18  21  24  27
4 │  4   8  12  16  20  24  28  32  36
5 │  5  10  15  20  25  30  35  40  45
6 │  6  12  18  24  30  36  42  48  54
7 │  7  14  21  28  35  42  49  56  63
8 │  8  16  24  32  40  48  56  64  72
9 │  9  18  27  36  45  54  63  72  81
```

1. The numbers at the eight vertices of one octagon are

```
          4    6
    3            12
    4            16
        10   15
```

Find the product of these 8 numbers. Is the product a square?

2. Find the product of the 8 numbers at the vertices of each of the other octagons indicated. What is true of the product in each case?

3. Draw in any other octagon of the same size as those shown in the table above. What is true of the product of the numbers at the vertices?

4. Each of the octagons shown in the table above is "equilateral." That is, each vertex is at a number adjacent to another vertex number. Suppose we were to draw larger octagons with the sides not necessarily the same length. We require only that each vertex be in the same row and column of the multiplication table as one of the other vertices.

For example, consider the octagon shown in this portion of the table.

```
 6    9   12   15   18   21   24
 8   12   16   20   24   28   32
10   15   20   25   30   35   40
12   18   24   30   36   42   48
```

The numbers in the 8 vertices are 9, 21, 32, 40, 42, 18, 10, and 8. Find their product. Is it a square?

5. Pick any octagon of any size that you wish. Multiply the numbers on the 8 vertices. Be certain that the octagon you pick is not lopsided. That is, be certain that each vertex is in the same row and column as one of the other vertices. What is true of the product of the 8 vertex numbers?

*****

Experiment Number 31

1. In this experiment we look at any two consecutive rows of the multiplication table. For our example, we have picked the multiples of 5 and of 6.

$$5 \diagup 10 \diagup 15 \diagup 20 \diagup 25 \diagup 30 \diagup 35 \diagup 40 \diagup 45$$
$$6 \diagup 12 \diagup 18 \diagup 24 \diagup 30 \diagup 36 \diagup 42 \diagup 48 \diagup 54$$

Find the differences between the two numbers along the diagonals indicated. To help get you started, the difference between 10 and 6 in the first diagonal is 4; the difference between 15 and 12 in the second diagonal is 3.   Find the difference between the two numbers on each of the other diagonals. What do you observe?

2. This time we use the multiples of 7 and 8.

$$7 \diagup 14 \diagup 21 \diagup 28 \diagup 35 \diagup 42 \diagup 49 \diagup 56 \diagup 63$$
$$8 \diagup 16 \diagup 24 \diagup 32 \diagup 40 \diagup 48 \diagup 56 \diagup 64 \diagup 72$$

Find the differences between the two numbers on the diagonals indicated.

3. Pick any two consecutive rows of the multiplication table. Find the differences between the pairs of numbers on the diagonal. What do you observe happening each time?

4. Next compute the consecutive differences between pairs of numbers on the diagonals in the opposite direction.

$$7 \diagdown 14 \diagdown 21 \diagdown 28 \diagdown 35 \diagdown 42 \diagdown 49 \diagdown 56 \diagdown 63$$
$$8 \diagdown 16 \diagdown 24 \diagdown 32 \diagdown 40 \diagdown 48 \diagdown 56 \diagdown 64 \diagdown 72$$

5. Select any two consecutive rows of the multiplication table and find the differences on the diagonals in the direction of those in question 4 above. What pattern do you notice?

*****

43

In this experiment we will investigate the sum of the numbers in the corner squares of the multiplication table.

x	1	2	3	4	5	6	7	8	9
1	1	2	3	4	5	6	7	8	9
2	2	4	6	8	10	12	14	16	18
3	3	6	9	12	15	18	21	24	27
4	4	8	12	16	20	24	28	32	36
5	5	10	15	20	25	30	35	40	45
6	6	12	18	24	30	36	42	48	54
7	7	14	21	28	35	42	49	56	63
8	8	16	24	32	40	48	56	64	72
9	9	18	27	36	45	54	63	72	81

1. The four numbers in the corners of the table are 1, 9, 9, and 81. What is their sum?

2. Next we find the sum of the numbers in each 2 by 2 cell, as marked. What is the sum of all 16 numbers in these four square cells? What is special about this sum?

x	1	2	3	4	5	6	7	8	9
1	1	2	3	4	5	6	7	8	9
2	2	4	6	8	10	12	14	16	18
3	3	6	9	12	15	18	21	24	27
4	4	8	12	16	20	24	28	32	36
5	5	10	15	20	25	30	35	40	45
6	6	12	18	24	30	36	42	48	54
7	7	14	21	28	35	42	49	56	63
8	8	16	24	32	40	48	56	64	72
9	9	18	27	36	45	54	63	72	81

3. Now find the sum of all 36 numbers in the four 3 by 3 corner squares. What pattern is emerging?

x	1	2	3	4	5	6	7	8	9
1	1	2	3	4	5	6	7	8	9
2	2	4	6	8	10	12	14	16	18
3	3	6	9	12	15	18	21	24	27
4	4	8	12	16	20	24	28	32	36
5	5	10	15	20	25	30	35	40	45
6	6	12	18	24	30	36	42	48	54
7	7	14	21	28	35	42	49	56	63
8	8	16	24	32	40	48	56	64	72
9	9	18	27	36	45	54	63	72	81

4. Predict the sum of the 64 numbers in the four 4 by 4 corner squares. What do you expect to be the sum of the 100 numbers in the four 5 by 5 corner squares?

*****

PATTERNS IN A TABLE OF SQUARES

Gratefully dedicated to the common postage stamp, without whose inspiration we might not have stuck with the Table of Squares until we found something interesting.

"Consider the postage stamp: its usefulness consists of its ability to stick to one thing until it gets there."
Josh Billings

Here is a table of squares of the numbers from 0 through 99.

	0	1	2	3	4	5	6	7	8	9
0	0	1	4	9	16	25	36	49	64	81
10	100	121	144	169	196	225	256	289	324	361
20	400	441	484	529	576	625	676	729	784	841
30	900	961	1024	1089	1156	1225	1296	1369	1444	1521
40	1600	1681	1764	1849	1936	2025	2116	2209	2304	2401
50	2500	2601	2704	2809	2916	3025	3136	3249	3364	3481
60	3600	3721	3844	3969	4096	4225	4356	4489	4624	4761
70	4900	5041	5184	5329	5476	5625	5776	5929	6084	6241
80	6400	6561	6724	6889	7056	7225	7396	7569	7744	7921
90	8100	8281	8464	8649	8836	9025	9216	9409	9604	9801

To use this table, find the tens digit along the left edge of the table and the units digit at the top of the table. The square is found at the intersection of the row and column in which those digits appear. Thus, the square of 56 can be found in the row headed 50 and the column headed 6. It is 3136. Similarly, the square of 83 is 6889.

Our experience with the addition and multiplication tables of the previous sections suggests that we might expect to find some interesting patterns buried in the table of squares. This is true, else this section would not be included in this book. However, as you are about to see, the patterns are generally of a different nature and are sometimes rather difficult to uncover.

1. The units digits of the entries in the first row are:

    0   1   4   9   6   5   6   9   4   1.

Notice that, except for the leading 0, the digits arrange themselves symmetrically around the center of the array. What are the final digits of the entries in the other rows?

2. Now look at the final two digits of each number in the first five rows.

00	01	04	09	16	25	36	49	64	81
00	21	44	69	96	25	56	89	24	61
00	41	84	29	76	(25)	76	29	84	41
00	61	24	89	56	25	96	69	44	21
00	81	64	49	36	25	16	09	04	01

The number at the center of this array is circled. (These are the last two digits of the square of 25, which is 625.) Notice that the other numbers distribute themselves symmetrically about that central number. That is, the two numbers on either side of 25 are each 76. The numbers appearing before and after 76 are each 29, and so forth.

3. Look next at the column of squares of numbers ending in 5.

$$25$$
$$225$$
$$625$$
$$1225$$
$$2025$$
$$3025$$
$$4225$$
$$5625$$
$$7225$$
$$9025$$

It is easy to see that each of these numbers ends in 25. But what can we say about the digits preceding 25? They are respectively

    0   2   6   12   20   30   42   56   72   90.

Divide each of these numbers by 2. Do you recognize the results? You certainly should!

4. Returning to the table of squares, examine the ten's digits of the entries in the column headed by 1. What pattern do you observe as you move down the column?

5.   Notice the ten's digits of the entries in the column headed
by 9. What pattern do you see as you move down that column?

6.   What can you say about the ten's digits in the column headed
by 6? In the column headed by 4?

*****

EXPERIMENT NUMBER 34

1.   Pick several entries in the table of squares and divide each
by 4. Record only the remainder of each division. What are the
possible remainders? Is the remainder ever 2 or 3?

2.   Divide several different entries in the table by 5 and record
only the remainder. Is the remainder ever 2 or 3?

3.   Divide several different entries in the table by 7. What are
the only possible remainders? Is the remainder ever 3, 5, or 6?

4.   What are the possible remainders if a square is divided by 8?
Is the remainder ever 2, 3, 5, 6, or 7?

5.   What remainders are possible when a square is divided by 16?
What is remarkable about these possible remainders?

*****

     At this point the patterns become more difficult to find and
it becomes tempting to paraphrase the Duchess. "Everything's got
a pattern, if you can only find it."

     "Tut, tut child!" said the Duchess. "Everything's got a
       moral, if you can only find it."

     Lewis Carroll: Alice's Adventures in Wonderland

47

1. In this experiment we will find the sums of numbers in blocks of cells from the table of squares.

	0	1	2	3	4	5	6	7	8	9
0	0	1	4	9	16	25	36	49	64	81
10	100	121	144	169	196	225	256	289	324	361
20	400	441	484	529	576	625	676	729	784	841
30	900	961	1024	1089	1156	1225	1296	1369	1444	1521
40	1600	1681	1764	1849	1936	2025	2116	2209	2304	2401
50	2500	2601	2704	2809	2916	3025	3136	3249	3364	3481
60	3600	3721	3844	3969	4096	4225	4356	4489	4624	4761
70	4900	5041	5184	5329	5476	5625	5776	5929	6084	6241
80	6400	6561	6724	6889	7056	7225	7396	7569	7744	7921
90	8100	8281	8464	8649	8836	9025	9216	9409	9604	9801

This table has been overlayed by several blocks. The four numbers in one of these blocks are

169 196
529 576.

Find the sum of these four numbers. There may seem to be nothing special about the sum; but subtract 101. Is the result a square?

2. Try this with other square blocks of four numbers. Find the sum of the four numbers; then subtract 101. What do you observe?

3. You will see another square block of nine numbers outlined in the table above. Those nine numbers are

676   729   784
1296 1369 1444
2116 2209 2304.

Find the sum of these 9 numbers; then subtract 606. What can you say about the result?

4. Select any block of 9 numbers, find their sum, and then subtract 606. What is true of the result?

5.   You also see a 4-cell "diamond" enclosed in the table. The numbers at the vertices of that diamond are


```
              4489
      5776            6084
              7569
```


Find the sum of these four numbers; then subtract 202. What is the result? Is it a square? Try this for other diamonds of your own choosing.

6. In another part of the preceding table, 5 numbers are enclosed by a cross. They are


```
              1764
      2601    2704    2809
              3844
```


Find their sum, subtract 202, and then divide by 5. What is the result? Is it a square?   Try this for other crosses; find the sums of the five numbers in the crosses; subtract 202; then divide by 5. Are the results always squares?

7. Here are four consecutive entries from one row of the table.


```
      225   256   289   324
```


Find their sum and then subtract 5. What is the answer? Is it a square?

8. Select any four consecutive entries from the table. Find their sum and then subtract 5. Is the result a square? Can you predict what that result will be?

9.   Pick any nine consecutive entries from the table of squares. Add them and then subtract 60. What is true of the result?

10.   Here are four consecutive numbers from a column.   576
Find their sum and then subtract 500. What can you say   1156
about the answer? Try this for any four consecutive   1936
entries in any column you choose. What do you always   2916
find?

*****

1. Select any two numbers on any diagonal from the table of squares in the direction of \\. (That is on a diagonal going from left to right as it moves down the table.) For example, suppose we pick 5329 and and 2601. Subtract the smaller from the larger. Is the difference divisible by 11?

	0	1	2	3	4	5	6	7	8	9
0	0	1	4	9	16	25	36	49	64	81
10	100	121	144	169	196	225	256	289	324	361
20	400	441	484	529	576	625	676	729	784	841
30	900	961	1024	1089	1156	1225	1296	1369	1444	1521
40	1600	1681	1764	1849	1936	2025	2116	2209	2304	2401
50	2500	2601	2704	2809	2916	3025	3136	3249	3364	3481
60	3600	3721	3844	3969	4096	4225	4356	4489	4624	4761
70	4900	5041	5184	5329	5476	5625	5776	5929	6084	6241
80	6400	6561	6724	6889	7056	7225	7396	7569	7744	7921
90	8100	8281	8464	8649	8836	9025	9216	9409	9604	9801

2. Select a variety of pairs of numbers along a diagonal as described in 1 above. Is the difference always divisible by 11?

3. Now select two numbers on any // diagonal, such as 625 and 4900. Is the difference a multiple of 9? Try this for several other choices of two numbers on the same // diagonal.

4. Our next exploration is a bit more complicated, but the results are quite surprising. Select any number from the table of squares...say 1764. Move down any number of rows...4 for example; and to the right, any number of columns...such as 2. In this example, starting in the table with 1764, moving down 4 and right 2, we see 7056. Now, we claim that the difference, 7056 - 1764 = 5292 is divisible by 42, a number whose digits are 4 and 2, the number of rows and columns we moved. Indeed 5292 divided by 42 is 126. Another example. Start with 441; move down 3 and over 7 to the right. The entry there is 3364. Is 3364 - 441 divisible by 37? Try it!

In general, you can pick a number from the Table of Squares and call it A. Choose another number R rows below and C columns to the right of A. Call it B. Find the difference, B - A. This difference is divisible by (10R + C). That is, (B - A) can be exactly divided by a number with ten's digit R and units digit C?

Try this for other entries of your choice.

*****

EXPERIMENT GROUP 3

PATTERNS IN PYTHAGOREAN TRIPLES

Gratefully dedicated to Major General Stanley, modern pirate fighter from Penzance, without whose teeming knowledge we would never have realized that hypotenuses are interesting in their own right.

"...and I'm teeming with a lot of news with many cheerful facts about the square of the hypotenuse."
Major General Stanley: <u>The Pirates of Penzance</u>, Gilbert and Sullivan

First we remind you of the famous Pythagorean theorem, sometimes called the right triangle theorem.

> PYTHAGOREN THEOREM: In any right triangle, the square on the hypotenuse is equal to the sum of the squares on the other two sides.

A frequently used illustration of this theorem is the 3-4-5 triangle. That is, the triangle measuring 3 cm and 4 cm on its two perpendicular sides (legs) and 5 cm on its hypotenuse is a right triangle.

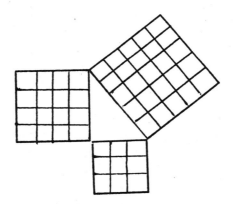

The area of the square on the 3 cm side is, of course, 9 cm^2; the square on the 4 cm side has an area of 16 cm^2; and the area of the square on the 5 cm hypotenuse is 25 cm^2. The Pythagorean theorem simply guarantees that

$$9 + 16 = 25.$$

In this experiment we investigate whether the regions constructed on each side of a right triangle must necessarily be squares. For example, could we put a semicircle on each side of the triangle instead of a square and expect the sum of the areas of the semicircles on the legs to equal the area of the semicircle on the hypotenuse?

1. A semicircle has been drawn on each side of this 3-4-5 right triangle.

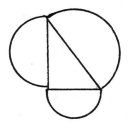

Find the area of each of the three semicircles. (You are reminded that the area of a semicircle is A = $\pi r^2/2$.) Is the area of the semicircle on the hypotenuse equal to the sum of the areas of the two semicircles on the legs of the triangle?

2. Suppose a regular hexagon is constructed on each side of the 3-4-5 right triangle. Find the area of each of the three

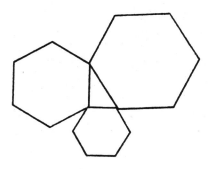

hexagons. (The formula for the area of a regular hexagon is

$$A = 2.598076s^2$$

where s is the length of each side of the hexagon.) Does the area of the hexagon on the hypotenuse equal the sum of the areas of the hexagons on the two sides?

3. Consider the 5-12-13 right triangle. If squares are drawn on each side of the triangle, does the theorem hold? What if semicircles are drawn on each side? Does the theorem still hold if hexagons are drawn on each side?

As you see, it is not necessary for the regions constructed on each side of a right triangle to be squares. It turns out, in fact, that the 3 regions may be any shape whatever, providing only that each is similar to the other two. But, since squares are easier to manage than most other simple closed curves, the rest of our experiments will refer only to the squares on each side. Thus, in any right triangle with perpendicular sides a and b and hypotenuse c,

$$a^2 + b^2 = c^2.$$

This implies that if we know two of the three sides of a right triangle, we can always find the third side.

*****

EXPERIMENT NUMBER 38

1. Using the notation that a and b are the lengths of the two perpendicular sides of a right triangle and that c is the length of the hypotenuse, find the side indicated in each of the following.

    (a) a = 8, b = 15. Find side c.
    (b) a = 21, c = 29. Find side b.
    (c) b = 39, c = 89. Find side a.

2. If a = 2 and b = 3. Find c. The nature of your answer is different from the answers to question 1 above. The hypotenuse, c, is equal to the square root of 13 which is approximately equal to 3.605551275. The square root of 13 is irrational which means that neither a fraction nor a decimal exists that is exactly equal to the square root of 13.

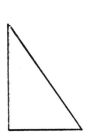

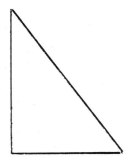

The 2-3-3.605551275
    right triangle.

The 3-4-5 right
    triangle.

54

While the

$$2\text{-}3\text{-}3.605551275$$

right triangle exists just as surely as does the

$$3\text{-}4\text{-}5$$

right triangle, we tend to favor the latter because all three sides are measured by whole numbers. Number triples such as (3,4,5) are referred to as Pythagorean triples. In the rest of this section we will understand that all three numbers of a Pythagorean triple are to be whole numbers. Otherwise we won't pay much attention to the triple.

3. Consider now these triples.

$$(3,4,5) \quad (6,8,10) \quad (9,12,15) \quad (12,16,20) \quad (15,20,25)$$

It is easy to verify that the sum of the squares of the first two numbers in each triple equals the square of the third number. Thus, each is a Pythagorean triple. For example in the triple (6,8,10)

$$6^2 + 8^2 = 36 + 64 = 100 = 10^2.$$

However, each member of (6,8,10) is double the corresponding member of (3,4,5). Similarly each member of (9,12,15) is 3 times the corresponding member of (3,4,5). In general, because (3,4,5) is a Pythagorean triple, so is (3k,4k,5k) for every value of k. Thus, once we discover one Pythagorean triple, we can immediately generate an infinity of additional triples simply by multiplying each element of the triple by any number we choose. This is summarized by stating that if (a,b,c) is a Pythagorean triple, then so is (ak,bk,ck).

A triple such as (3,4,5) is called a PRIMITIVE PYTHAGOREAN TRIPLE. In any primitive triple no two elements will have a common factor. From each primitive triple we can generate as many other triples as we please by multiplying the elements of the triple by any constant. It is the primitive triples that we find the most interesting.

*****

EXPERIMENT NUMBER 39

1. Verify that each of the following is a primitive Pythagorean triple.

$$(3,4,5) \quad (5,12,13) \quad (7,24,25) \quad (9,40,41) \quad (11,60,61)$$

$$(13,84,85) \quad (15,112,113) \quad (17,144,145) \quad (19,180,181)$$

2. The first elements of successive triples in question 1 are 3, 5, 7, 9, 11, etc.; that is, they are consecutive odd numbers. In the triple (a,b,c) we can pick any odd number for a and expect to find b and c to complete the triple. Given a, an odd number in the triple (a,b,c) try to find a rule that will enable us to find b and c. (Hint: In the triple (5,12,13) what is the sum of 12 and 13? How is that sum related to 5? In each of the other triples shown in question 1, how is the sum of b and c related to a? How are b and c related?

3. Construct triples (a,b,c) in which a = 21, 23, 25, 27, and 29.

4. We are currently considering only one class of Pythagorean triples. In this class of triples, (a,b,c), b and c differ by 1. Given any odd number a, what are the formulas for b and c?

*****

EXPERIMENT NUMBER 40

1. Here are some primitive Pythagorean triples.

    (3,4,5)   (5,12,13)   (7,24,25)   (8,15,17)   (9,40,41)

    (20,21,29)   (12,35,37)   (11,60,61)   (16,63,65)   (33,56,65)

    (48,55,73)   (36,77,85)   (13,84,85)   (39,80,89)   (20,99,101)

    (60,91,109) (15,112,113)   (44,117,125)   (88,105,137)   (51,140,149)

The third, and largest, element of each triple represents the hypotenuse of the right triangle. Does it appear that this third element, c, is always an odd number?

2. In any primitive triple, how many of the elements appear to be odd numbers? How many of the elements are even numbers?

3. If an element of a triple is an even number, is it divisible by 4? Does every primitive triple appear to have an element that is divisible by 4? What conjecture can you make?

4. Check through each triple listed in question 1 and determine whether one of the elements is divisible by 3. Based upon your findings, make a conjecture.

5. Is c, the hypotenuse, ever divisible by 3? Is c ever divisible by 4? Make a conjecture.

6. Check through each triple listed above and determine whether one of the elements is divisible by 5. What is your conjecture?

7. Multiply the three elements of any primitive Pythagorean triple. What is the largest number that will divide every such product?

8. Now restrict b of the triple (a,b,c) to be the even number. Thus, a and c are odd, with c the hypotenuse. Find the sum of b + c for each triple listed in question 1. What is true of that sum?

9. Again with b the even element, what appears to be true about the difference c - b in any primitive Pythagorean triple?

10. Consider now the sum of the two odd elements a + c of the primitive triple (a,b,c). After finding the sum of a and c, divide by 2. What can you say about the result?

11. Find the difference between the two odd elements of any primitive triple and divide by 2. That is, for each triple evaluate (c - a)/2. What appears to be true?

12. A very old, well-known method for generating Pythagorean triples follows. Pick any two whole numbers m and n with m > n, such that one of the numbers chosen is even and the other is odd.

$$\text{Let } a = m^2 - n^2$$

$$b = 2mn$$

$$c = m^2 + n^2$$

Then (a,b,c) is a Pythagorean triple.

Select values of m and n to generate other Pythagorean triples.

13. Using the formulas given in question 12 above, what happens if m and n are both even or both odd? What happens if m and n have a common factor? For example, suppose that m = 9 and n = 3.

14. Prove that the formulas given in question 12 above will indeed always generate a Pythagorean triple.

*****

EXPERIMENT NUMBER 41

1. In this experiment we generate a variety of different classes of primitive Pythagorean triples. We will continue to use the following notation for every primitive triple (a,b,c).

a is an odd number and is the length of one leg.

b is an even number and is the length of the other leg.

c is an odd number and is the length of the hypotenuse.

In Experiment 39 we looked at a class of primitive triples in which c exceeds b by 1. Some of those triples are:

(3,4,5) (5,12,13) (7,24,25) (9,40,41) (11,60,61)

Recall also that in Experiment 40 we gave you a formula to generate Pythagorean triples. Pick any whole numbers for m and n with m > n. (If m and n are not both odd and if they do not have a common factor, then the resulting triple (a,b,c) will be a primitive triple.) Let

$$a = m^2 - n^2$$

$$b = 2mn$$

$$c = m^2 + n^2$$

If we wish to generate triples (a,b,c) in which c = b + 1, what rule should we follow in choosing m and n?

2. What are the possible values of c - a if (a,b,c) is a primitive Pythagorean triple? Using the generating formula,

$$c - a = (m^2 + n^2) - (m^2 - n^2) = 2n^2.$$

Since possible values of n^2 are

1 4 9 16 25 36 49 64 100 121 144 169 196 etc.

what are the possible values of c - a ?

3. Since c - a may equal 2, we will now find examples of such triples. To generate the class of primitive triples in which c - a = 2, choose n = 1 because c - a = $2n^2$. Select an even number for m. Thus,

m	n	a	b	c
2	1	3	4	5
4	1	15	8	17
6	1	35	12	37
8	1	63	16	65
10	1	99	20	101

Generate several more primitive triples in which c - a = 2.

4. In question 2 we also discovered that c - a may equal 8. If c - a = 8, then $2n^2 = 8$, which means that n = 2. Picking odd values for m, when n = 2, we can generate triples in which side a and the hypotenuse c differ by 8.

m	n	a	b	c
3	2	5	12	13
5	2	21	20	29
7	2	45	28	53
9	2	77	36	85

Generate five more primitive triples in which c - a = 8.

5. If we select n = 3 and m an even number, not divisible by 3, we will generate primitive triples in which c - a = 18. (If m is divisible by 3, such as in m = 6, then c - a will equal 18, but the triple will not be primitive.) The chart below demonstrates this fact.

m	n	a	b	c	
4	3	7	24	25	
6	3	27	36	45	(A "multiple" of 3-4-5.)
8	3	55	48	73	
10	3	91	60	109	
12	3	135	72	153	(A "multiple" of 15-8-17.)

Generate several more primitive triples in which c - a = 18.

6. We have seen that c - a can also equal 32, 50, 72, 98, and any other number of the form $2n^2$. Generate four or five triples of each of these classes.

*****

EXPERIMENT NUMBER 42

In this experiment we are interested in discovering which numbers can appear in a primitive Pythagorean triple and which numbers cannot.

1. Consider again the results of Experiment 39. Is it possible to generate a primitive triple involving any positive odd number we wish? What about a = 1?

2. The even number b is found using the formula

$$b = 2mn.$$

If one of m or n is even and the other is odd, then what number divides every value of b?

3. Is every multiple of 4 a member of a primitive triple?

4. If every odd number and every multiple of 4 is a leg of some primitive triple, what are the only whole numbers which are never members of primitive triples?

5. Many odd numbers appear as the leg in only one primitive triple (a,b,c). For example, the only triple in which a = 13 is (13,84,85). However, a is 15 in two different primitive triples, (15,112,113) and (15,8,17); a = 105 in four different primitive triples. They are

(105,88,137) (105,208,233) (105,608,617) (105,5512,5513).

What property must the number a have so that it will appear as the odd side in more than one primitive Pythagorean triple? Hint: Note that

$$a = m^2 - n^2 = (m - n)(m + n).$$

If a is prime, then its factors, (m - n) and (m + n), must equal 1 and a, respectively. What if a is a composite number?)

6. In question 3 we decided that any multiple of 4 can appear as b in a primitive triple. It happens that most multiples of 4 appear in more than one primitive triple, but a few multiples of 4 appear in only one. For example, the only primitive triple containing 32 is (255,32,257). On the other hand, 60 appears in four different primitives. They are

(11,60,61) (91,60,109) (221,60,229) (899,60,901).

Recalling that b = 2mn and that exactly one of m or n must be odd, can you decide which multiples of 4 can appear in only one primitive triple? Which multiples of 4 will appear in exactly two primitive triples?

*****

EXPERIMENT NUMBER 43

1. 840 is a very popular number among Pythagorean triples because it appears in 68 different triples. However, most of these triples are not primitive. In only one of these triples is 840 equal to the hypotenuse, c. That triple is (504,672,840). Since 168 is a common factor of each of these elements, this triple is a "multiple" of (3,4,5).

"I'm really very popular in my set! I am a member of 68 sets of Pythagorean triples. I think that's <u>very</u> impressive!"

In the other 67 triples in which 840 appears, 840 is one of the legs. Find as many as you can of the 67 Pythagorean triples (a,b,c) in which either a or b is equal to 840. (Remember that a must be odd only in primitive triples. In this experiment we are looking for all Pythagorean triples in which 840 is one of the legs, primitive or not.) To do this, you will need to find all divisors of 840; then find primitive triples involving those

60

divisors. Next, multiply each member of each such triple by whatever is necessary to make either a or b equal 840.

For example, 21 divides 840. A triple involving 21 is (21,20,29). Multiplying each member of this triple by 40 we have the triple (840,800,1160). Each of the other triples involving 840 can be found in a similar manner.

2. There is a fairly simple method (but it looks complicated) for determining in how many Pythagorean triples a given number n will appear either as a or as b. The formulas are quite easy to use; they just look difficult. We use one formula if n is even and a slightly different formula if n is odd.

Whether n is even or odd, first factor n into its prime factors.

CASE I. If n is even, then its prime factors are in the form

$$n = 2^e p^f q^g r^h ...$$

where p, q, r, etc. are prime numbers. The even number n will appear as a or b in k different Pythagorean triples (a,b,c) where

$$k = ([(2e - 1)(2f + 1)(2g + 1)(2h + 1)...] - 1)/2.$$

CASE II. If n is odd, then its prime factors are of the form

$$n = p^f q^g r^h ...$$

where p, q, r, etc. are primes. The odd number n will appear as a in k different Pythagorean triples (a,b,c) where

$$k = ([(2f + 1)(2g + 1)(2h + 1)...] - 1)/2.$$

We used case I to determine that there are 67 Pythagorean triples in which either a or b is 840. First, we factored 840 into its prime factors.

$$840 = 2^3 \times 3^1 \times 5^1 \times 7^1$$

Thus, k =([5 x 3 x 3 x 3] - 1)/2 = (135 - 1)/2 = 134/2 = 67.

NOTE: A careful reader who counts all the triples in which 840 appears either as a or as b will find 68 triples, not 67. However, this count includes (840,800,1160) in which a = 840 as well as the triple (800,840,1160) in which b = 840. Since these are really equivalent triples, we have counted them only once.

In how many triples does each of the following numbers appear as either a or b?

(a) 100   (b) 120   (c) 720   (d) 7500   (e) 23100

(f) 1155   (g) 17325

3. What number less than 1000 do you think appears in the greatest number of Pythagorean triples?

4. Recall that 4! (read 4 factorial) = 1 x 2 x 3 x 4 = 24, and that 5! = 1 x 2 x 3 x 4 x 5 = 120. In how many Pythagorean triples would we expect to find 12! as one of the legs?

5. In how many triples is 30! one of the legs? We won't try to list all such triples in the answer section. Answer the following questions to see why. If a computer could print one such triple each second, how long would it require to print all the triples in which 30! is one of the legs? If the printout from the computer lists the triples one under the other, 6 triples per inch, how far would the printout stretch?

*****

EXPERIMENT NUMBER 44

In Experiments 42 and 43 we confined our attention to a and b, the legs of the right triangle. In this experiment we will look at possible values of c, the hypotenuse.

1. Recall that $c = m^2 + n^2$. If c is to be the hypotenuse of a primitive triple we require (a) that m and n do not have a common factor and (b) that m and n not both be odd.

Thus, one of the numbers must be even, the other odd. However, if m = 9 and n = 6, even though m is odd and n is even, since they have 3 as a common factor, they will not generate a primitve triple. (That triple is (45,108,117), a multiple of the primitive triple (5,12,13).)

To find the possible values for c we prepare an addition table showing the sums of m^2 and n^2. This table will help get you started.

TABLE OF HYPOTENUSES

		m^2			
+	4	16	36	64	100
1	5	17	37	65	101
9	13	25	*	73	109
25	29	41	61	89	*
49	53	65	85	113	149
81	85	97	*	145	181

(leftmost column labeled n^2)

The asterisks (*) in the table replace the sum of $m^2 + n^2$ wherever m and n have a common factor. In this experiment we are interested only in primitive triples.

Continue building the table in this manner and find all possible values for c less than 350. This may seem like quite a bit of work, but we need a lot of numbers to help in the discoveries which will soon follow.

62

2. A careful examination of the table in question 1 shows that some numbers appear more than once. For example 65 appears as the sum of 49 + 16 as well as 64 + 1. This means that 65 is the hypotenuse of two different primitive triples. In one triple m and n are 7 and 4; in the other they are 8 and 1, and the triples involving 65 are (33,56,65) and (63,16,65). What other numbers less than 350 appear more than once in the extension of the table of question 1? Generate the primitive Pythagorean triples to which they belong.

3. In question 1, if you found all possible values of c less than 350, then these numbers appeared twice in your table.

$$65 \quad 85 \quad 145 \quad 185 \quad 205 \quad 221 \quad 265 \quad 305 \quad 325$$

Are these numbers prime or composite? If they can be factored, find the prime factors of each number.

4. The results for question 3 seem to imply that numbers appearing twice in the table are all composite numbers. Does that mean that numbers appearing only once are prime numbers? Here are the numbers less than 350 that appear in the table only once.

5	13	17	25	29	37	41	53	61	73	89
97	101	109	113	125	137	149	157	169	173	181
193	197	229	233	241	257	269	277	281	289	293
313	317	337	349							

Are there any numbers appearing in the table only once that are not prime numbers?

5. Your answer to question 4 should have been that some composite numbers appear only once. They are

$$25 \quad 125 \quad 169 \quad 289.$$

What can you say about the factors of these numbers?

6. Look carefully at the prime factors of the composite numbers in question 3. What conjecture can we make? Based on the very limited sample of numbers in question 5, what conjecture might we make about composite numbers that appear only once in the table of hypotenuses?

7. It appears that if c_1 and c_2 are two different prime numbers in two different primitive triples

$$(a_1,b_1,c_1) \quad \text{and} \quad (a_2,b_2,c_2)$$

then the product, c_1c_2 appears as the hypotenuse in two different primitive triples. Can you prove this algebraically?

8. We next build a limited multiplication table. The multipliers used in the table are the first six numbers that can equal c, the hypotenuse. These six multipliers are

$$5 \quad 13 \quad 17 \quad 29 \quad 37 \quad 41.$$

Now here's the multiplication table.

x	5	13	17	29	37	41
5	25	65	85	145	185	205
13		169	221	377	481	533
17			289	493	629	697
29				841	1073	1189
37					1369	1517
41						1681

Take a careful look at the products shown in this multiplication table. We remind you again that the multipliers shown in the margins of the tables are prime numbers that can be the hypotenuses of right triangles. But, what about the products shown in the table? Those products are not prime, but each is a number that can be a hypotenuse. Moreover, the entries that are not squares must appear as hypotenuses in at least two different right triangles. For example, 65 is a product shown in the table and 65 is the hypotenuse in two different primitive triples, (33,56,65) and (63,16,65).

The conclusion is interesting. The set of possible hypotenuse lengths is closed under multiplication. This simply means that the product of 2 possible hypotenuse lengths is another possible hypotenuse. Moreover, if a composite number is to be a hypotenuse of a right triangle, then each of its prime factors must also be a hypotenuse.

As another example, triangles with hypotenuses of 13 and 17 exist. Thus, since 13 x 17 = 221, there exist two primitive right triangles in which 221 is the hypotenuse. They are (21,220,221) and (171,140,221).

"We Hypotenuses belong to a very exclusive closed club,
you know! Membership is denied to any length that is
not the product of other members of our set."

"That makes us very regal indeed, but perhaps we
are somewhat inbred."
*****

EXPERIMENT NUMBER 45

1.   Pick any Pythagorean triple (a,b,c). Form two fractions from
the members of this triple, c/a and c/b. Square each. Compare the
sum of these squares with their product.

For example, pick (3,4,5). The two fractions are 5/3 and
5/4; their squares are 25/9 and 25/16.

The sum is 25/9 + 25/16 = 400/144 + 225/144 = 625/144.

The product is 25/9 x 25/16 = 625/144.

Surprisingly, the sum and product are equal.

2. Select any other Pythagorean triple, (a,b,c). Does the sum

$$c^2/a^2 + c^2/b^2$$

equal the product

$$c^2/a^2 \text{ x } c^2/b^2 \text{ ?}$$

Try several more triples. Had you thought that 2 and 2 were the
only pair of numbers with a product equal to their sum?

3. Can you prove this fact algebraically?

*****

We know, of course, that if a rectangle measures 3 cm by 4 cm, then its diagonal is 5 cm. The Pythagorean theormen tells us that. Suppose now we have a rectangular solid in three dimensions measuring 3 cm by 4 cm by 12 cm. How long is the diagonal of that rectangular solid?

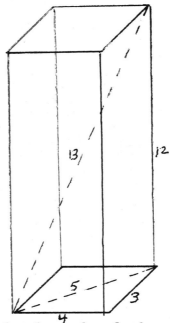

It is easy to show that the length of the diagonal d can be found from the expression

$$d^2 = 3^2 + 4^2 + 12^2$$

$$= 9 + 16 + 144 = 169.$$

Thus, $d = 13.$

In general, if a rectangular solid measures a, b, and c on its 3 edges, then the diagonal d is given by

$$d^2 = a^2 + b^2 + c^2$$

Just as we call (a,b,c) a Pythagorean triple, we refer to (a,b,c,d) as a Pythagorean quadruple. In the example above, we saw our first Pythagorean quadruple (3,4,12,13).

A person who is quite familiar with Pythagorean <u>triples</u> may be unaware of very many <u>quadruples</u> and incorrectly assume that Pythagorean quadruples are relatively rare and difficult to find. Quite to the contrary! Pythagorean quadruples abound and can be easily generated. In this experiment we will discover a method to generate Pythagorean quadruples that include just about any numbers we wish to select.

1. Verify that each of the following quadruples is a primitive Pythagorean quadruple.

(1,2,2,3) (1,4,8,9) (1,6,18,19) (2,3,6,7) (2,5,14,15)

(2,7,26,27) (3,4,12,13) (4,7,32,33) (4,4,7,9)

(6,6,7,11) (6,6,17,19) (4,5,20,21) (10,10,23,27)

2. Here is one way to generate a Pythagorean quadruple, (a,b,c,d). Since we require that

$$a^2 + b^2 + c^2 = d^2,$$

this means that

$$a^2 + b^2 = d^2 - c^2 = (d - c)(d + c).$$

This suggests that we are free to pick any values we wish for a and b; one should be even, the other odd. It is always possible to factor

$$a^2 + b^2$$

into two odd factors even if $a^2 + b^2$ is prime. In that case the two odd "factors" are 1 and the number itself. Next, set d - c equal to the smaller of the two factors and d + c equal to the larger factor. Solve for c and d and lo and behold...there's a Pythagorean quadruple!

For example, suppose we pick a = 5 and b = 8. We are to find c and d so that

$$5^2 + 8^2 + c^2 = d^2.$$

Thus, $\qquad 5^2 + 8^2 = 89 = d^2 - c^2$

and $\qquad 89 = 1 \times 89 = (d - c)(d + c).$

Therefore, (d - c) = 1 and (d + c) = 89. Solving for c and d, we have c = 44 and d = 45. The resulting Pythagorean quadruple is

(5,8,44,45).

Generate some Pythagorean quadruples of your own.

*****

EXPERIMENT GROUP 4

SOME SUMS AND PRODUCTS

Gratefully dedicated to Captain Corcoran and to Little Buttercup, named respectively ruler of the Queen's navy and in honor of a species of ranunculus (though neither never knew why), without whose careful scrutiny of the commonplace, we might never have scrutinized the computations presented in this experiment group.

> "Things are seldom what they seem.
> Skim milk masquerades as cream."

Captain Corcoran and Little Buttercup: H.M.S. Pinafore, Gilbert and Sullivan

In this series of experiments you will discover several interesting computational patterns. Alas! Some of the patterns are not destined to extend forever. But others shall!

EXPERIMENT NUMBER 47

1. Find the answers to each of the following.

   (a) $(9 \times 9) + 7 =$

   (b) $(98 \times 9) + 6 =$

   (c) $(987 \times 9) + 5 =$

   (d) $(9876 \times 9) + 4 =$

   (e) $(98765 \times 9) + 3 =$

   (f) $(987654 \times 9) + 2 =$

   (g) $(9876543 \times 9) + 1 =$

   (h) $(98765432 \times 9) + 0 =$

   (i) $(987654321 \times 9) - 1 =$

   (j) $(9876543210 \times 9) - 2 =$

The pattern is clear. But what comes next? That's not so clear. Actually, it turns out that

$$(98765432099 \times 9) - 3 = 888\ 888\ 888\ 888 \quad \text{and}$$

$$(987654320988 \times 9) - 4 = 8\ 888\ 888\ 888\ 888.$$

As we extend the computations, a new pattern for the multipliers of 9 is being established. If you have a lot of patience and persistence you are invited to try to find that new pattern.

2. Here is another sequence.

(a) (1 x 9) + 2 =

(b) (12 x 9) + 3 =

(c) (123 x 9) + 4 =

(d) (1234 x 9) + 5 =

(e) (12345 x 9) + 6 =

3. Continue the pattern of multiplication as long as possible. What do you expect (123456789 x 9) + 10 to equal?

It is not obvious what the multiplier of 9 should be in the step that follows next. To find that factor it will be necessary to find a number, n, such that

$$(n \times 9) + 11 = 11 \ 111 \ 111 \ 111.$$

The solution to this equation is n = 1 234 567 900. This is the first entry of a new, modified pattern. Can you find that pattern?

4. Find the answer to each of the following.

(a) (1 x 8) + 1 =

(b) (12 x 8) + 2 =

(c) (123 x 8) + 3 =

(d) (1234 x 8) + 4 =

(e) (12345 x 8) + 5 =

Continue the pattern as long as you can.

5. Here is still another pattern for you to discover. Evaluate each of the following.

(a) (9 x 1) - 1 =

(b) (9 x 21) - 1 =

(c) (9 x 321) - 1 =

(d) (9 x 4321) - 1 =

(e) (9 x 54321) - 1 =

Continue the pattern as long as you can.

*****

In this experiment we will examine the squares of 11, 111, 1 111, etc.

1. Evaluate each of the following.

(a) 11^2 (b) 111^2 (c) $1\ 111^2$

(d) $11\ 111^2$ (e) $111\ 111^2$ (f) $1\ 111\ 111^2$

(g) $11\ 111\ 111^2$ (h) $111\ 111\ 111^2$

2. It is not clear what the square of 1 111 111 111 might be. Square this number and see what happens. A new pattern is being established. See if you can discover it.

3. If you are especially persistent, you may find it interesting to square numbers such as 111 111 111 111 111 111 111 and even larger numbers.

*****

EXPERIMENT NUMBER 49

This experiment examines some permanent patterns.

1. Evaluate each of the following.

(a) $9^2 - 2^2$

(b) $89^2 - 12^2$

(c) $889^2 - 112^2$

(d) $8\ 889^2 - 1\ 112^2$

(e) $88\ 889^2 - 11\ 112^2$

2. What do you predict to be the answer to

$888\ 888\ 888\ 888\ 889^2 - 111\ 111\ 111\ 111\ 112^2$?

3. Now try these computations.

(a) 37 x 3

(b) 37 x 33

(c) 37 x 333

(d) 37 x 3 333

(e) 37 x 33 333

(f) 37 x 333 333

4. Predict the product of 37 x 333 333 333 333 333 333 333 333.

5. Finally, find these products.

    (a) 9 x 7   (b) 99 x 67   (c) 999 x 667

    (d) 9 999 x 6 667   (e) 99 999 x 66 667

    (f) 999 999 x 666 667   (g) 9 999 999 x 6 666 667

*****

EXPERIMENT NUMBER 50

1. In the first part of this experiment we will find the product of two consecutive counting numbers and then add .25. Evaluate each of the following.

    (a) (1 x 2) + .25   (b) (2 x 3) + .25

    (c) (3 x 4) + .25   (d) (4 x 5) + .25

    (e) (5 x 6) + .25   (f) (6 x 7) + .25

2. Each of the decimal fractions computed in question 1 is a square. Find the square root of each.

3. Examine the patterns in your answers and decide what will be the square roots of   (a)   (157 x 158) + .25.
(b) (2113 x 2114) + .25.

4. Go back to your answers to question 1. From each answer, subtract .25, the decimal part. Then divide by 2. What can you say about the results?

5. State the law for the square root of [n x (n + 1)] + .25.

6. Next multiply pairs of numbers differing by 2; then add 1.

    (a) (1 x 3) + 1   (b) (2 x 4) + 1

    (c) (3 x 5) + 1   (d) (4 x 6) + 1

    (e) (5 x 7) + 1   (f) (6 x 8) + 1

7. What do you observe about each answer in question 6?

8. (64948 x 64950) + 1 is equal to the square of what number?

9. In general [n x (n + 2)] + 1 is the square of what number?

10. In the next sequence we multiply two numbers differing by 3 and then add 2.25.

    (a) (1 x 4) + 2.25   (b) (2 x 5) + 2.25

    (c) (3 x 6) + 2.25   (d) (4 x 7) + 2.25

    (e) (5 x 8) + 2.25   (f) (6 x 9) + 2.25

11. Each answer in question 10 is, of course, a decimal fraction. Is each answer a square?

12. Study the pattern of answers in question 10. We would expect the square of what number to equal (20 x 23) + 2.25?

13. To generalize, the square of what number is equal to

$$[n \times (n + 3) + 2.25]?$$

14. Before continuing, it may be helpful to summarize the patterns discovered in questions 1, 6, and 10.

DIFFERENCE BETWEEN FACTORS	NUMBER ADDED TO PRODUCT
1	$.25 = .5^2$
2	$1 \quad = 1^2$
3	$2.25 = 1.5^2$

15. Are you ready to predict what number should be added if the difference between the factors is 4?

Find these values to confirm your conjecture.

    (a) (1 x 5) + 4   (b) (2 x 6) + 4

    (c) (3 x 7) + 4   (d) (4 x 8) + 4

    (e) (5 x 9) + 4   (f) (6 x 10) + 4

16. The square of what number is equal to (50 x 54) + 4?

17. From the patterns established in questions 14 and 15, in general what is the value of

$$[n \times (n + 4)] + 4 ?$$

18. Finally, we summarize the results of Experiment 50. Complete the blanks in the following equation?

$$[n \times (n + k)] + \underline{\hspace{2cm}} = \underline{\hspace{2cm}}$$
$$\overline{*****}$$

72

EXPERIMENT NUMBER 51

In this experiment we investigate the product of four numbers plus a constant addend.

1. Evaluate each of the following.

   (a) $(1 \times 2 \times 3 \times 4) + 1$ (b) $(2 \times 3 \times 4 \times 5) + 1$

   (c) $(3 \times 4 \times 5 \times 6) + 1$ (d) $(4 \times 5 \times 6 \times 7) + 1$

   (e) $(5 \times 6 \times 7 \times 8) + 1$ (f) $(6 \times 7 \times 8 \times 9) + 1$

2. Is each result in question 1 equal to a square?

3. Can you predict the result of

   (a) $(10 \times 11 \times 12 \times 13) + 1$?   (b) $(20 \times 21 \times 22 \times 23) + 1$?

4. In general, what is the value of

   $$[n \times (n + 1) \times (n + 2) \times (n + 3)] + 1?$$

5. What happens if the factors differ by 2? Evaluate each of the following.

   (a) $(1 \times 3 \times 5 \times 7) + 16$ (b) $(2 \times 4 \times 6 \times 8) + 16$

   (c) $(3 \times 5 \times 7 \times 9) + 16$ (d) $(4 \times 6 \times 8 \times 10) + 16$

   (e) $(5 \times 7 \times 9 \times 11) + 16$ (f) $(6 \times 8 \times 10 \times 12) + 16$

6. Predict the value of each of the following. Then check to see if your prediction is correct.

   (a) $(20 \times 22 \times 24 \times 26) + 16$ (b) $(50 \times 52 \times 54 \times 56) + 16$

7. Complete the following.

   $$[n \times (n + 2) \times (n + 4) \times (n + 6)] + 16 =$$

8. If the four factors each differ by 3, we must add 81 if the result is to be a square. Try these.

   (a) $(1 \times 4 \times 7 \times 10) + 81$ (b) $(2 \times 5 \times 8 \times 11) + 81$

   (c) $(3 \times 6 \times 9 \times 12) + 81$ (d) $(4 \times 7 \times 10 \times 13) + 81$

   (e) $(5 \times 8 \times 11 \times 14) + 81$ (f) $(6 \times 9 \times 12 \times 15) + 81$

9. Predict the result of $(40 \times 43 \times 46 \times 49) + 81$.

10. In general, what is the value of

   $$[n \times (n + 3) \times (n + 6) \times (n + 9)] + 81?$$

11. Try to summarize the results of this experiment by filling in the blanks of the following equation.

$$[n \times (n + k) \times (n + 2k) \times (n + 3k)] + \underline{\hspace{2cm}} = \underline{\hspace{2cm}}$$

*****

EXPERIMENT NUMBER 52

"A mathematician, like a painter or a poet, is the maker of patterns. If his patterns are more permanent than theirs, it is because they are made with ideas."
Godfrey Harold Hardy: A Mathematician's Apology

Many numbers have rather surprising square roots. In this experiment we look at several.

1. Find the square root of each of the following, rounded down to the nearest whole number.

    (a) 11   (b) 1 111   (c) 111 111

    (d) 11 111 111   (e) 1 111 111 111

2. What do you think is the greatest integer in the square root of 111 111 111 111 111 111 111 111?

3. Find the square root of these numbers rounded down to the nearest whole number.

    (a) 44   (b) 4 444   (c) 444 444

    (d) 44 444 444   (e) 4 444 444 444

4. Make a conjecture about the greatest integer in the square root of 444 444 444 444 444 444 444 444 444 444.

5. Now try these square roots rounded down to the nearest whole number.

    (a) 544   (b) 54 444   (c) 5 444 444

    (d) 544 444 444

6. Using the patterns established in question 5, what do you expect to be the square root of

       544 444 444 444 444 444 444 444 444 444 444 ?

7. Find these square roots, rounding down to the nearest whole number.
    (a) 177   (b) 711   (c) 17 777   (d) 71 111

    (e) 1 777 777   (f) 7 111 111

    (g) 177 777 777   (h) 711 111 111

8. Rounded down to the nearest whole number, what are the square roots of

(a) 1 777 777 777 777 777 777 777 777 777 777 ?

(b) 7 111 111 111 111 111 111 111 111 111 111 ?

9. Find these square roots rounded down to the nearest whole number.

(a) 277　　(b) 27 777　　(c) 2 777 777　　(d) 277 777 777

10. What is the square root of

2 777 777 777 777 777 777 777 777 777 777 777 777 ?

11. The rather surprising squares and square roots we worked with in questions 1 to 10 are only a few of many such possibilities. As it turns out, they are easy to find and easy to explain. The underlying explanation behind all of such squares and square roots depends upon these three simple facts.

(i) The square root of 1/9 is 1/3.

(ii) The decimal value of 1/9 is 0.111111111111...

(iii) The decimal value of 1/3 is 0.333333333333...

It immediately follows that the square root of 0.11111111111... is 0.33333333333... .

Note also that if the square root of n is r, then the square root of 100n is 10r; and in general the square root of

$$10^{2k}n \quad is \quad 10^{k}r.$$

This means that the square root of 11111111.111111... must equal 3333.333...; from which it follows that the square root of the whole number 11111111 to the nearest whole number is 3333.

Now do you see where this leads? We need only to start with any improper fraction of the form

$$n^2/9.$$

Its square root is n/3. For example, the decimal value of 16/9 is 1.7777777777...; the square root of 16/9 is 4/3 and that decimal value is 1.3333333333... . It follows then that the greatest integer square root of 17777777777 is 133333.

12. Generate more squares and square roots with repeating digits similar to those shown in questions 1 to 10. We have seen that the numbers that may act as repetends in the squares are 1, 4, and 7. Are these the only numbers that will appear as repetends? What numbers can appear as repetends in the square roots?

EXPERIMENT NUMBER 53

The first part of this experiment can be used as a magic trick.

1. Select any 3-digit number. (All three digits should not be the same.) As an example, we'll choose 285; you choose any other 3-digit number that you wish.

2. Reverse the digits of the number chosen. 582.

3. Subtract the smaller of these two numbers from the larger.

$$582 - 285 = 297$$

4. Reverse the digits of the difference and add.

$$297 + 792 = 1089.$$

5. Our answer is 1089. What is your answer?

6. Select another 3-digit number and go through these steps again. What is your answer?

7. If you make no mistakes, the answer will always be 1089, no matter what 3-digit number you start with, providing the digits are not all the same. (We need to be careful in the case of selecting a number such as 293. In this case 392 - 293 = 99. We must treat this 2-digit difference as if it were a 3-digit number, that is treat it as 099. Then when we reverse the digits and add we have 099 + 990 = 1089.)

8. Try this on your friends as a magic trick. Write the final answer, 1089, on a slip of paper and seal it in an envelope. After your friend has selected a 3-digit number (without telling you the number picked) and has done the computations, hand him or her the envelope which will reveal the answer when opened. Alas! This trick can be performed only once per person since the answer is always 1089.

9. 1089 has some interesting properties. Perform the indicated multiplications and examine the answers carefully.

(a) 1089 x 1 = _____   and   1089 x 9 = _____

(b) 1089 x 2 = _____   and   1089 x 8 = _____

(c) 1089 x 3 = _____   and   1089 x 7 = _____

(d) 1089 x 4 = _____   and   1089 x 6 = _____

(e) 1089 x 5 = _____

What is true of each pair of answers?

10. Here are some more pairs of multipliers of 1089 with interesting results.

    (a) 1089 x 12 = _____   and   1089 x 79 = _____

    (b) 1089 x 13 = _____   and   1089 x 69 = _____

    (c) 1089 x 14 = _____   and   1089 x 59 = _____

    (d) 1089 x 15 = _____   and   1089 x 49 = _____

    (e) 1089 x 23 = _____   and   1089 x 68 = _____

    (f) 1089 x 24 = _____   and   1089 x 58 = _____

    (g) 1089 x 37 = _____   and   1089 x 36 = _____

11. Try to find more such pairs.

12. Consider again 1089 and its reverse 9801. Both of these numbers are squares. What are their square roots? Can you discover other numbers such that both the number and its reverse are squares. (Consider, for example 169 and 961.) How many others can you find?

*****

EXPERIMENT NUMBER 54

In this experiment we investigate some of the rare attributes of the number 142857.

1. Find each of the following products. Look carefully at each answer.

    (a) 142857 x 2 =

    (b) 142857 x 3 =

    (c) 142857 x 4 =

    (d) 142857 x 5 =

    (e) 142857 x 6 =

2. If you made no mistakes, each answer in question 1 is a cyclic permutation of 142857. That is, each answer uses only the digits 142857 in that order, except that the cycle begins in a different place each time. But, what can we expect to be the result of

142857 x 7 ?

Try it. You might be surprised!

3. (a) Find the sum of the digits of 142857; that is, find the sum of 1 + 4 + 2 + 8 + 5 + 7; then find the sum of the digits of your answer.

(b) Next, find the sum of the the digits of 142857 taken two at a time. That is, find the sum of 14 + 28 + 57.

(c) Now, find the sum of 142 + 857.

(d) Find the sum of the 1st and 4th digits of 142857; that is, find the sum of 1 + 8. Next find the sum of the 2nd and 5th digits of 142857; finally find the sum of the 3rd and 6th digits.

4. The first 3 digits of 142857 are 142. Increased by 1, the number is 143. Now select any other sequence of 3 digits in 142857 or in any of its cylcic permutations and increase that 3-digit number by 1. The 3-digit sequences are

142   428   285   857   571   714.

Increased by 1 these numbers are

143   429   286   858   572   715.

Is each of these 3-digit numbers (after adding 1) divisible by 143, the first number in the list?

5. There exists an infinite quantity of other numbers with similar properties to 142857, but most of these numbers are so large that computation with them becomes quite tedious. The next such number is 588,235,294,117,647. When this number is multiplied by each whole number from 1 to 16, the product is a cyclic permutation of 0588235294117647. What do you think the product will be when 588,235,294,117,647 is multiplied by 17? Try it.

*****

EXPERIMENT NUMBER 55

In our final experiment we examine the rather interesting number

12345679.

1. This number, in itself, is interesting because it is made up of all the single-digit counting numbers, in order, except for 8. Moreover, the square root 123456790 may be quite a surprise to you. If you can enter a 10-digit number in your calculator, enter 123456790 and press the square root button. What is the answer? (If you don't have a calculator that will accept 10-digit numbers, then you will need to peek at the answer in the back of the book.) If you know how to extract square root by hand and have an extreme amount of patience you will find some real surprises if you carry the square root of 123456790 to many places after the decimal.

2. Find each of the following products and fill in the blanks.

   (a) 12345679 x 1 = _____. Missing digits are 0 and 8.

   (b) 12345679 x 2 = _____. Missing digits are 0 and ___.

   (c) 12345679 x 4 = _____. Missing digits are 0 and ___.

   (d) 12345679 x 5 = _____. Missing digits are 0 and ___.

   (e) 12345679 x 7 = _____. Missing digits are 0 and ___.

   (f) 12345679 x 8 = _____. Missing digits are 0 and ___.

3. Perhaps you wondered why you weren't asked to multiply 12345679 by 3, by 6, or by 9 in question 2. The reason is that the answers don't conform to the patterns established in that question. Nevertheless, the products are not without a pattern as you shall now discover.

   (a) 12345679 x 3 = _____

   (b) 12345679 x 6 = _____

   (c) 12345679 x 9 = _____

4. Multiples of 12345679 x 9 develop some interesting and predictable patterns. Try these multiplications and see how soon you can predict the pattern of the answers. (How are you expected to find these answers if your calculator only displays 8-digit numbers? It is not as much work as it might seem because the product of the first two factors, 12345679 x 9, is 111 111 111. The next step of multiplying 111 111 111 by the third factor isn't so tough if you have to do it with pencil and paper.)

   (a) 12345679 x 9 x 11 = 1 222 222 221

   (b) 12345679 x 9 x 12 = 1 333 333 332

   (c) 12345679 x 9 x 13 = _ ___ ___ ___

   (d) 12345679 x 9 x 14 = _ ___ ___ ___

   (e) 12345679 x 9 x 15 = _ ___ ___ ___

   (f) 12345679 x 9 x 21 = _ ___ ___ ___

   (g) 12345679 x 9 x 53 = _ ___ ___ ___

   (h) 12345679 x 9 x 62 = _ ___ ___ ___

   (i) 12345679 x 9 x 71 = _ ___ ___ ___

5. Try other multiples of 12345679 x 9 of your own choosing. However, at this stage the multiplier should be a 2-digit number such that the sum of the two digits is 9 or less. When such a number is multiplied by 12345679 x 9, what is the nature of the product? Can you state the rule?

6. If the sum of the digits of the 2-digit multiplier is greater than than 9, the pattern is just a bit more complicated. Try these products.

   (a)   12345679 x 9 x 28 = 3 111 111 108

   (b)   12345679 x 9 x 29 = 3 222 222 219

   (c)   12345679 x 9 x 37 = 4 111 111 107

   (d)   12345679 x 9 x 38 = _ ___ ___ ___

   (e)   12345679 x 9 x 39 = _ ___ ___ ___

   (f)   12345679 x 9 x 46 = _ ___ ___ ___

   (g)   12345679 x 9 x 47 = _ ___ ___ ___

   (h)   12345679 x 9 x 59 = _ ___ ___ ___

   (i)   12345679 x 9 x 87 = _ ___ ___ ___

7. State a rule for the product of 12345679 x 9 times a 2-digit number less than 90 if the sum of the two digits is more than 9.

8. Investigate the product of 12345679 x 9 times numbers in the 90's. What happens if 12345679 x 9 is multiplied by 3-digit numbers?

*****

Experiment 1.

2. Yes. T(8) + T(9) = 36 + 45 = 81, which is the square of 9.

3. T(16) + T(17) = 136 + 153 = 289 = 17^2. The sum is a square.

4. T(24) + T(25) = 300 + 325 = 625. The sum is the square of 25.

5. The pattern established in the earlier steps of this experiment suggests that the sum is the square of 88.

6. Yes. The sum of any two consecutive triangles is a square. Can you prove this fact algebraically?

7. T(n) + T(n+1) = $(n+1)^2$.

Experiment 2.

2. T(6) = 21; 21 x 8 = 168; 168 + 1 = 169; yes, 169 = 13^2.

3. T(11) = 66; (8 x 66) + 1 = 529; yes, 529 = 23^2.

4. Yes. [8T(n)] + 1 is always a square. Can you prove it algebraically?

5. 8T(n) + 1 = $(2n+1)^2$.

Experiment 3.

1. The three sums are 16, 25, and 36, the squares of 4, 5, and 6.

2. The sum is 100, the square of 10.

3. 400 = 20^2; 10,000 = 100^2.

4. The sum of the first n odd numbers is n^2.

Experiment 4.

2. The squares of 10 and 15 are 100 and 225; the sum is 325. Yes, 325 is a triangular number; it is the triangle of 25; and 25 is a square.

3. The sum of the squares of any two consecutive triangular numbers is the triangle of a square.

4. $[T(n)]^2 + [T(n+1)]^2 = T[(n+1)^2]$.

Experiment 5.

2. Yes. $45^2 - 36^2 = 2025 - 1296 = 729 = 9^3$.

3.   Yes. The difference between the squares of two consecutive triangles is a cube.

4. $[T(n+1)]^2 - [T(n)]^2 = (n+1)^3$.

Experiment 6.

2. $T(1) + T(4) - 2 = 1 + 10 - 2 = 9 = 3^2$.
   $T(2) + T(5) - 2 = 16$; $T(3) + T(6) - 2 = 25$;
   $T(7) + T(10) - 2 = 81$; $T(8) + T(11) - 2 = 100$;
   $T(9) + T(12) - 2 = 121$.

3. Yes. $T(n) + T(n + 3) - 2 = (n + 2)^2$.

5.   The results are 36, 49, 64, 81, 529, and 9216 respectively. These are the squares of 6, 7, 8, 9, 23, and 96.

7.   The results are 25, 36, 49, 64, 529, and 1681. These are the squares of 5, 6, 7, 8, 23, and 41.

8. Yes.

9. The results are squares.

11.   The three missing entries in the table are 30, 42, and 56. Each of these numbers is twice a triangular number.

Experiment 7.

1. No. $(n^2)/(n+1)^2$ can never be reduced to lower terms if n is a positive whole number.

2. Yes; yes. $T(n)/T(n+1)$ can always be reduced if n is a positive whole number greater than 1.

3. Yes.

4. Yes. The lowest common denominator is a triangular number.

Experiment 8.

1. The result is a triangular number.

2. The result is the square of a triangular number.

3. The result is the cube of a triangular number.

4. Yes.

Experiment 9.

1. Yes. One is positive, the other negative.

2. The sum is -1.

3. 0 and -1.

4. 1 and -2.

5. Each solution is -1/2. Thus, the "two" triangular roots of -1/8 are -1/2 and -1/2, just as the "two" square roots of 0 are 0 and 0.

6. No. The triangular roots of numbers less than -1/8 are complex numbers. For example, the triangular roots of -13/4 are (-1 + 5i)/2 and (-1 - 5i)/2.

7. Yes. Both of these roots are negative. For example, the triangular roots of -3/32 are -1/4 and -3/4. Their sum is -1, of course.

Experiment 10.

1. The difference between consecutive polygonal powers of 4 is 6.

2. 10, 15, and 21. These are triangular numbers.

3. We would expect the differences to be $T(19) = 190$.

4. $T(n-1)$.

Experiment 11.

1. The respective sums are 15, 25, 35, 45, 55, and 65. These sums are the triangle, the square, the pentagon, the hexagon, the heptagon, and the octagon of 5.

2. The sum of the first 6 counting numbers is $21 = T(6)$. The sum of first 6 odd numbers is 36, the square of 6. The sum of the six numbers $1 + 4 + 7 + 10 + 13 + 16$ is 51, the pentagon of 6. In general, $1 + (1+n) + (1+2n) + (1+3n) + (1+4n) + (1+ 5n) = [(n+2)-gon](6)$.

3. The sum is $P(20) = 590$.

4. The sum is $H(50) = 4950$.

5. The sum is $[(d+2)-gon](n) = (n/2)[2 + (n-1)d]$.

Experiment 12.

2. The sum is 51, which is the pentagon of 6.

3. The sum is 66, which is the hexagon of 6.

4. Yes. $2T(n) + T(n+1) = P(n+1)$.

5. $3T(n) + T(n+1) = H(n+1)$.

6. $4T(n) + T(n+1) = [7\text{-gon}](n+1)$.

7. $kT(n) + T(n+1) = [(k+3)\text{-gon}](n+1)$.

Experiment 13.

1. $H(5) = 45$, which is also $T(9)$.

2. $T(19) = H(10) = 190$.

3. Every hexagonal number is also a triangular number.

4. $H(n) = T(2n-1)$.

5. The difference is a triangular number. In fact, $P(n) - n^2 = T(n-1)$.

6. The difference is a triangular number. $H(n) - P(n) = T(n-1)$.

7. The difference is $T(n-1)$.

8. The result is the hexagon of n.

9. The result is a square. In fact, $3[8\text{-gon}](n) + 1 = (3n-1)^2$.

10. The result is the square of the number picked.

Experiment 14.

1. (a) 1   (b) 9   (c) 36   (d) 100   (e) 225
   (f) Subsequent sums are 441, 784, 1296, 2025, and 3025.

2. Each square root is a triangular number.

3. (a) 1   (b) 28   (c) 153   (d) 496.   (e) Subsequent sums are 1225, 2556, 4753, and 8128.

4. The sums are not squares, but they are triangles.

5. The results are 9 and 36, squares of 3 and 6, which in turn are triangular numbers.

Experiment 15.

1. (a) 7   (b) 19   (c) 37   (d) 61.   (e) The next several such differences are 91, 127, 169, and 217.

2. The results are 1, 3, 6, 10, 15, 21, 28, and 36, and these numbers are consecutive triangular numbers.

3. (a) 9   (b) 35   (c) 91   (d) 189.   (e) The next several such sums are 341, 559, 855, and 1241. If you cannot spot a pattern see question 4 of this experiment.

4. The final results are 1, 3, 6, 10, 15, 21, 28, and 36, and these numbers are consecutive triangular numbers.

5. (a) 17 (b) 97 (c) 337 (d) 881 (e) Subsequent sums are 1921, 3697, 6497, 10657, and 16561.

6. The results are 1, 6, 21, 55, 120, 231, 406, 666, and 1035. These numbers are triangles, but they are not consecutive triangles. In fact, they are the triangles of 1, 3, 6, 10, 15, 21, 28, 36, and 45, which are also triangles. Thus, the sum of the fourth powers of two consecutive counting numbers minus 1 and divided by 16 is the triangle of a triangle!

7. (a) 15 (b) 65 (c) 175 (d) 369 (e) The next several such differences are 671, 1105, 1695, and 2465.

8. The final results are 1, 3, 6, 10, 15, 21, 28, and 36, and these numbers are consecutive triangular numbers.

Experiment 16.

1 (a) 4 (b) 12 (c) 24 (d) 40 (e) Subsequent results are 60, 84, 112, and 144.

2. The results are 1, 3, 6, 10, 15, 21, 28, and 36, and these numbers are triangular numbers.

3. (a) 18 (b) 90 (c) 252 (d) 540.

4. The results are triangles.

5. (a) 14 (b) 38 (c) 74 (d) 122

6. The results are triangles.

Experiment 17.

1.

n					
4	16	136	10	100	36
5	25	325	15	225	100
6	36	666	21	441	225
7	49	1225	28	784	441
8	64	2080	36	1296	784
9	81	3321	45	2025	1296
10	100	5050	55	3025	2025

2. The entries in the final column are squares of triangles.

3.

n				
4	64	16	80	48
5	125	25	150	100
6	216	36	252	180
7	343	49	392	294
8	512	64	576	448
9	729	81	810	648
10	1000	100	1100	900

4. The results are all triangular numbers.

5. (a) 1 (b) -3 (c) 6 (d) -10. (e) The next several such answers are 15, -21, 28, -36, and 45. The answers are triangular numbers with alternating signs.

6. (a) 1 (b) 28 (c) 153 (d) 496. (e) Subsequent sums are 1225, 2556, 4753, and 8128. Each is a triangular number.

7. $1 = 1^2 \times 1$; $28 = 2^2 \times 7$; $153 = 3^2 \times 17$;

$496 = 4^2 \times 31$; $1225 = 5^2 \times 49$; $2556 = 6^2 \times 71$;

$4753 = 7^2 \times 97$; $8128 = 8^2 \times 127$.

The multipliers of the squares are 1, 7, 17, 31, 49, 71, 97, and 127. If 1 is added to each of these numbers and the sum then divided by 2, the results are 1, 4, 9, 16, 25, 36, 49, and 64, and these numbers are square numbers.

8 and 9.

n							
4	256	16	240	= 4	x 6	x 10	
5	625	25	600	= 4	x 10	x 15	
6	1296	36	1260	= 4	x 15	x 21	
7	2401	49	2352	= 4	x 21	x 28	
8	4096	64	4032	= 4	x 28	x 36	
9	6561	81	6480	= 4	x 36	x 45	
10	10000	100	9900	= 4	x 45	x 55	

*****

RESULTS OF THE EXPERIMENT GROUP 2

Experiment 18.

1. The sum is 45.

2. The sum is 55.

3. The sum is 65.

4. The sums of the subsequent rows are respectively 75, 85, 95, 105, 115, 125, and 135. The sums increase by 10.

Experiment 19.

3.   The sum is 27.

4.   The sums are 36, 45, 54, 63, 72, 81, and 90. They are consecutive multiples of 9.

6.   The sums are 12, 20, 30, 42, 56, 72, and 90. If the diagonal sums are divided by 2 the results are 0, 1, 3, 6, 10, 15, 21, 28, 36, and 45. These are consecutive triangular numbers.

Experiment 20.

2.   The sum is 28, and 28 = 4 x 7.

3.   The sum is 52, and 52 = 4 x 13.

4.   The sum of 5, 6, 6, and 7 is 24, and 24 = 4 x 6. The sum of the block with 9, 10, 10, and 11 is 40, and 40 = 4 x 10. Finally, the sum of the block with 14, 15, 15, 16 is 60, and 60 = 4 x 15.

5.   The sum is always 4 times the repeated number.

Experiment 21.

1. The sum is 36, and 36 = 9 x 4.

2. The sum is 72, and 72 = 9 x 8.

3. The sum is 126, and 126 = 9 x 14.

4. The sum is the product of 9 and the repeated number on the center diagonal.

5. The sum is 144, and 144 = 16 x 9.

6. The sum is the product of 16 times the repeated number on the center diagonal.

7. There are 100 numbers in the block; the number on the diagonal is 9, so the sum must be 100 x 9 = 900.

Experiment 22.

2. The sum is 20.

3. The sum in the upper cross is 40; in the lower cross the sum is 50.

4. The sums are the products of 5 and the numbers in the centers of the crosses.

5. The sum is 91.

6. The sum is the product of 7 and the number in the center of the H.

7. The four sums are 23, 28, 48, and 73.

8. One rule is that the sum is equal to the product of 5 and the number in the center of T's cross, plus 3. Another rule is that the sum is the product of 5 times the number at the foot of the T, minus 7. Can you find other rules?

9. One rule is that the sum is 9a - 5, where a is the number located at the left foot of M.

Experiment 23.

2. Cross products are 49 and 45. The difference is 49 - 45 = 4.

3. Each difference is 4.

4. The difference is always 4. Note that $4 = 2^2$.

6. $(49 \times 45) + 4 = 2209 = 47^2$.

7. The other products increased by 4 are: $3844 = 62^2$; $9604 = 98^2$; $20164 = 142^2$; and $64516 = 254^2$.

8. If the number in the center of the X is n, the result is
$$S = (n^2 - 2)^2.$$

Experiment 24.

1. In each case the difference is 9, and $9 = 3^2$.

2. The differences should always be 9.

3. The cross products are 64 and 48; their difference is 16.

4. The difference is $(n - 1)^2$.

Experiment 25.

1. The sum is 36; $36 = 6^2$.

2. The sum is 144; $144 = 12^2$.

3. The sum is 324; $324 = 18^2$.

4. In steps 1, 2, and 3 the sums are the squares of 6, 12, and 18. These are consecutive multiples of 6. Thus, we would expect the sum of the 64 numbers in the four 4 by 4 blocks to total the square of 24, or 576.

5. The next multiple of 6 is 30; the sum should be 30^2 = 900. Compare this result with your answer to step 7 in Experiment Number 21.

Experiment 26.

2.   7 + 16 + 27 = 50

3.   The respective sums are 80, 115, 154, 196, 240, and 285.

4.   9 x 3/27 = 1; 26 x 3/26 = 3; 50 x 3/25 = 6; 80 x 3/24 = 10; 115 x 3/23 = 15; 154 x 3/22 = 21; 196 x 3/21 = 28; 240 x 3/20 = 36; and 285 x 3/19 = 45. Each product is a triangular number.

Experiment 27.

1. The sums are 10, 20, 35, 56, 84, 120, and 165.

2. 1 x 3/3 = 1; 4 x 3/4 = 3; 10 x 3/5 = 6; 20 x 3/6 = 10; 35 x 3/7 = 15; 56 x 3/8 = 21; 84 x 3/9 = 28; 120 x 3/10 = 36; and 165 x 3/11 = 45. Each product is a triangular number.

3. 10 x 6 = 60 = 3 x 4 x 5; 20 x 6 = 120 = 4 x 5 x 6; 35 x 6 = 210 = 5 x 6 x 7; 56 x 6 = 336 = 6 x 7 x 8; 84 x 6 = 504 = 7 x 8 x 9; 120 x 6 = 720 = 8 x 9 x 10; 165 x 6 = 990 = 9 x 10 x 11.

Experiment 28.

2.   All fractions reduce to 2/5.

3.   To reduce 12/30 to lowest terms, find a 12 and a 30 that appear in the same column in the table. The numbers which head the rows in which 12 and 30 appear are 2 and 5 respectively. Thus, 12/30 reduces to 2/5.

Experiment 29.

1. 2 x 6 x 3 x 9 = 324 = 18^2.

2. 14 x 18 x 35 x 45 = 396,900 = 630^2.

3. 5 x 10 x 8 x 16 = 6400 = 80^2;

   15 x 25 x 27 x 45 = 455,625 = 675^2;

   48 x 72 x 54 x 81 = 15,116,544 = 3888^2.

4.   The product is the square of the product of the two vertex numbers at opposite ends of either diagonal.

5. In the case of 112 = 7 x 16, the vertices appear in rows 2 and 5 and in columns 7 and 9. The sum of the rows, 2 + 5 = 7, is one factor; and the sum of the columns, 7 + 9 = 16, is the other factor.

Experiment 30.

1. 4 x 6 x 12 x 16 x 15 x 10 x 4 x 3 = 8,294,400 = 2880^2.

2. 7 x 8 x 18 x 27 x 32 x 28 x 18 x 12 =
$$5,267,275,776 = 72,576^2;$$
36 x 42 x 56 x 64 x 63 x 54 x 40 x 35 =
$$25,809,651,302,400 = 5,080,320^2.$$

3. The product is a square.

4. 9 x 21 x 32 x 40 x 42 x 18 x 10 x 8 =
$$14,631,321,600 = 120,960^2.$$
5. The product is a square.

Experiment 31.

1. The differences are 4, 3, 2, 1, 0, -1, -2, and -3.

2. The differences are 6, 5, 4, 3, 2, 1, 0, and -1.

3. Moving from left to right, the differences decrease by 1.

4. The differences are 9, 10, 11, 12, 13, 14, 15, and 16.

5. Reading from left to right, the differences increase by 1.

Experiment 32.

1. 1 + 9 + 9 + 81 = 100 = 10^2.

2. The sum is 400, and 400 is a square because 400 = 20^2.

3. The sum is 900, and 900 is a square. 900 = 30^2. Each sum, so far, is a square.

4. The sums are 1600 = 40^2; and 2500 = 50^2.

Experiment 33.

1. The final digits of each entry in every row are

        0   1   4   9   6   5   6   9   4   1.

3. After dividing by 2 the results are

        0   1   3   6   10   15   21   28   36   45.

These are consecutive triangular numbers.

90

4. The ten's digits are 0,   2,   4,   6,   8,   0,   2, 4, 6, 8; they increase by 2 (mod 10).

5.   The ten's digits are 8,   6,   4,   2,   0,   8, 6, 4, 2, 0; they decrease by 2.

6.   In the column headed by 6 the ten's digits are the increasing odd numbers (mod 10) 3,   5, 7, 9, 1, 3, 5, 7, 9, 1. In the column headed by 4 the ten's digits are 1,   9,   7,   5, 3, 1, 9, 7, 5, 3, decreasing odd numbers (mod 10).

Experiment 34.

1. If a square is divided by 4 the remainder is either 0 or 1, never 2 or 3.

2. If a square is divided by 5 the remainder is 0, 1, or 4, never 2 or 3.

3. If a square is divided by 7 the remainder is 0, 1, 2, or 4, never 3, 5, or 6.

4. If a square is divided by 8 the remainder is 0, 1, or 4, never 2, 3, 5, 6, or 7.

5. If a square is divided by 16 the remainder is 0, 1, 4, or 9 (all squares), never 2, 3, 5, 6, 7, 8, 10, 11, 12, 13, 14, or 15.

Experiment 35.

1. The sum is 1470; 1470 - 101 = 1369 = 37^2.

2. Each such result is a square.

3. The sum is 12927; 12927 - 606 = 12321 = 111^2.

4. The result is a square.

5. The sum is 23918; 23918 - 202 = 23716 = 154^2.

6. The sum is 13722; 13722 - 202 = 13520; 13520/5 = 2704 = 52^2.

7. The sum is 1094; 1094 - 5 = 1089 = 33^2.

8. Yes. The result is the square of the sum of the square roots of the two end numbers.

9. The result is a square.

10. The sum is 6584; 6584 - 500 = 6084 = 78^2.

Experiment 36.

1. 5329 - 2601 = 2728; 2728/11 = 248.

2. The difference is always divisible by 11.

3. 4900 - 625 = 4275; 4275/9 = 475. The differences are always divisible by 9.

4. Yes. 3364 - 441 = 2923; 2923/37 = 79.

*****

RESULTS OF EXPERIMENTS IN EXPERIMENT GROUP 3

Experiment 37.

1. The area of the semicircle on side of length 3 is 3.5343 cm^2, the area on side of length 4 is 6.2832 cm^2, and the area on the side of length 5 is 9.8175 cm^2. Yes, 3.5343 + 6.2832 = 9.8175.

2. The areas of the hexagons on sides 3, 4, and 5 are respectively 23.3827 cm^2, 41.5692 cm^2, and 64.9519 cm^2. Yes, 23.3827 + 41.5692 = 64.9519.

3. Yes. Squares: 25 + 144 = 169.
   Semicircles: 9.8175 + 56.5487 = 66.3662.
   Hexagons: 64.9519 + 374.1229 = 439.0748.

Experiment 38.

1. (a) c = 17;   (b) b = 20;   (c) a = 80.

2. c = $\sqrt{13}$ = 3.605551275 (approximately). This is an irrational number. The answers to problem 1 were all rational.

Experiment 39.

2. The difference between b and c in each case is 1. The sum of b and c is a^2.

3. (21,220,221);(23,264,265);(25,312,313);(27,364,365); (29,420,421).

4. If a is odd, b = $(a^2 - 1)/2$; c = $(a^2 + 1)/2$.

Experiment 40.

1. Yes. In any primitive triple c is odd.

2. Two of the elements are odd; one is even.

3. Yes, 4 divides the even element of any primitive triple.

4. Either a or b, but not both, is always divisible by 3.

5. The hypotenuse, c, in a primitive triple is never divisible by 3 or 4. Moreover, it can be shown that neither 7 nor 11 will ever divide the hypotenuse of a primitive triple.

6. Yes, 5 divides exactly one of the numbers a, b, or c in any primitive Pythagorean triple.

7. $60 = 3 \times 4 \times 5$ divides the product of the three elements of any Pythagorean triple.

8. In any primitive triple, c + b is a square.

9. In any primitive triple, c - b is a square.

10. In any primitive triple, (c + a)/2 is square.

11. In any primitive triple (c - a)/2 is a square.

12. As an example, if m = 7 and n = 4, then a = 33; b = 56; and c = 65. (33,56,65) is a primitive triple.

13. If m and n are both odd or if they have a common factor, then the triple generated will not be a primitive triple.

14. $a^2 + b^2 = (m^2 - n^2)^2 + (2mn)^2$

$$= m^4 - 2m^2n^2 + n^4 + 4m^2n^2$$

$$= m^4 + 2m^2n^2 + n^4$$

$$= (m^2 + n^2)^2 = c^2.$$

Experiment 41.

1. If c - b = 1, then $(m^2 + n^2) - 2mn = 1$. That is,

$$m^2 - 2mn + n^2 = (m - n)^2 = 1.$$

This simply requires that m - n = 1. In other words, choose n to be any whole number we please; then let m = n + 1.

2. Possible values of c - a are 2, 8, 18, 32, 50, 72, 98, etc.

3. Two other triples with c - a = 2 are (143,24,145) and (195,28,197).

4. Five more triples in which c - a = 8 are (117,44,125), (165,52,173), (221,60,229), (285,68,293), and (357,76,365).

5. Two such triples are (187,84,205) and (247,96,265).

6. As an example, if c - a = 50, then $2n^2 = 50$ and n = 5. Choose any even m > 5 (that is not also a multiple of 5). If m = 8, then the triple generated is (39,80,89).

Experiment 42.

1. Every odd number appears as a in at least one primitive Pythagorean triple. For odd a, the triple that certainly can be generated is

$$(a,[a^2 - 1]/2,[a^2 + 1]/2).$$

If a = 1, the triple so generated is (1,0,1), the trivial case.

2. The even element of a primitive Pythagorean triple is divisible by 4.

3. Yes. Since b = 2mn, we can always find an m and an n such that one is odd and the other even. For example, if b = 20, then

$$2mn = 20$$
$$or \quad mn = 10.$$

We are free to choose m = 10 and n = 1, or m = 5 and n = 2. Thus, there are two primitives in which 20 appears. They are (99,20,101) and (21,20,29).

4. Even numbers not divisible by 4 are never members of a primitive Pythagorean triple. These include such numbers as

2   6   10   14   18   22   26   30   34   etc.

5. Odd prime numbers appear as a leg in exactly one primitive triple. Composite odd numbers appear in as many primitive triples as there are ways to factor the number into two relatively prime factors. 105 appears in 4 primitive triples because

$$105 = 1 \times 105 = 53^2 - 52^2 \qquad 105 = 3 \times 35 = 19^2 - 16^2$$

$$105 = 5 \times 21 = 13^2 - 8^2 \qquad 105 = 7 \times 15 = 11^2 - 4^2.$$

Each factoring leads to a different m^2 and n^2. (Don't forget that a = $m^2 - n^2$.) For a = 105, since there are 4 sets of values of m and n, we can generate four different primitive triples.

6. Powers of 2 will appear in only one primitive triple. For example, 64 which is a power of 2 when set equal to 2mn gives us

$$2mn = 64$$

$$mn = 32.$$

Since one of m or n must be odd and the other even, the only choices we have for m and n are m = 32 and n = 1. Thus the only primitive triple in which 64 is a member is (1023,64,1025).
The multiples of 4 which can appear in exactly two triples are those which factor to the form

$$2^n p$$

where p is a prime (not 2.) For example $40 = 2^3$ x 5 appears in exactly two primitive triples because if

$$2mn = 40$$

then

$$mn = 20.$$

The possible solutions for m and n (remembering that one must be odd and the other even) are m = 5 and n = 4, or m = 20 and n = 1. These lead to the triples (9,40,41) and (399,40,401).

Here's another example to help convince you. Suppose we decide we want the even leg to have the factor 2 repeated many times, such as in 1792. The factors of 1792 are

$$2^8 \text{ x } 7.$$

Since

$$2mn = 1792$$

then

$$mn = 896 = 2^7 \text{ x } 7.$$

If one of the factors m or n must be odd, that odd factor can only be 1 or 7. So, there are only 2 Pythagorean triples with 1792 as the even leg. The two are (16335, 1792, 16433) and (802815, 1792, 802817).

Experiment 43.

1. Following are the 67 Pythagorean triples (a,b,c) in which b = 840.

41	840	841	1274	840	1526	5005	840	5075
58	840	842	1350	840	1590	5850	840	5910
130	840	850	1463	840	1687	6272	840	6328
154	840	854	1575	840	1785	7031	840	7081
189	840	861	1664	840	1864	7326	840	7374
245	840	875	1702	840	1898	8379	840	8421
288	840	888	1870	840	2050	8800	840	8840
306	840	894	2016	840	2184	9782	840	9818
350	840	910	2125	840	2285	11009	840	11041
448	840	952	2277	840	2427	11745	840	11775
475	840	965	2378	840	2522	12586	840	12614
495	840	975	2450	840	2590	14688	840	14712
559	840	1009	2737	840	2863	17630	840	17650
630	840	1050	2880	840	3000	19591	840	19609
682	840	1082	3094	840	3206	22042	840	22058
704	840	1096	3478	840	3578	25193	840	25207
800	840	1160	3551	840	3649	29394	840	29406
833	840	1183	3627	840	3723	35275	840	35285
882	840	1218	3875	840	3965	44096	840	44104
1026	840	1326	4158	840	4242	58797	840	58803
1053	840	1347	4370	840	4450	88198	840	88202
1081	840	1369	4864	840	4936	176399	840	176401
1120	840	1400						

2. (a) 100 appears as a or b in 7 triples. (b) 120 is in 22 triples. (c) 720 is in 52 triples. (d) 7500 is in 40 triples. (e) 23100 appears in 202 triples. (f) 1155 is in 40 triples. (g) 17,325 appears in 112 triples.

3. Probably 840 appears in more Pythagorean triples than any other number less than 1000.

4. $12! = 479,001,600 = 2^{10} \times 3^5 \times 5^2 \times 7 \times 11$ and thus appears as one of the legs of a right triangle in 4702 triples.

5. $30! = 2^{26} \times 3^{14} \times 5^7 \times 7^4 \times 11^2 \times 13^2 \times 17 \times 19 \times 23 \times 29$. Therefore, 30! is a leg in 202,160,812 right triangles. If the computer were to print out one triple per second, it would require 6 years and 5 months to print every triple containing 30!. The printout would be nearly 532 miles long. We will refrain from listing all these triples.

Experiment 44.

1. This table shows all hypotenuses less than 350, along with several that are greater than 350.

+	4	16	36	64	100	144	196	256	324
1	5	17	37	65	101	145	197	257	324
9	13	25	*	73	109	153	205	265	*
25	29	41	61	89	*	169	221	281	349
49	53	65	85	113	149	193	*	305	373
81	85	97	*	145	181	*	277	337	*
121	125	137	157	185	221	265	317	377	445
169	173	185	205	233	269	313	365	425	493
225	229	241	*	289	*	*	421	481	*
289	293	305	325	356	393	433	485	545	613

The results for this question are found in questions 3, 4, and 5 of this experiment.

2. The results for this question are found in question 3 of this experiment.

3. Each number is composite. 65 = 5 x 13; 85 = 5 x 17; 145 = 5 x 29; 185 = 5 x 37; 205 = 5 x 41; 221 = 13 x 17; 265 = 5 x 53; 305 = 5 x 61; and 325 = 5 x 5 x 13.

4. Yes. Numbers appearing only once that are not primes are 25, 125, 169, and 289.

5. Each of these four numbers is either a square or a cube of a prime number appearing in the table.

96

6. From examining the table we might conclude that:

    (a)   the only composite numbers appearing in the table of hypotenuses are factorable into primes appearing in that table.

    (b)   composite numbers, other than powers of a single prime, appear twice in the table.

    (c)   composite numbers that are powers of primes found in the table are also in the table, but appear only once.

7. If $m^2 + n^2 = c_1$ and $p^2 + q^2 = c_2$, then

$$c_1 c_2 = (m^2 + n^2)(p^2 + q^2)$$
$$= m^2 p^2 + m^2 q^2 + n^2 p^2 + n^2 q^2.$$

Subtracting and adding $2mnpq$, we have

$$= m^2 p^2 - 2mnpq + n^2 q^2 + m^2 q^2 + 2mnpq + n^2 p^2.$$

Thus, $c_1 c_2 = (mp - nq)^2 + (mq + np)^2$.

In a similar manner $c_1 c_2 = (mp + nq)^2 + (mq - np)^2$ also.

Therefore, we conclude that if c_1 is the sum of two squares and if c_2 is the sum of two other squares, then the product $c_1 c_2$ can be expressed as the sum of two squares in two different ways.

To complete the proof that each of the triples in which $c_1 c_2$ is the hypotenuse is a primitive triple, it is necessary to show that $(mp - nq)$ and $(mq + np)$ are mutually prime; and that $(mq - np)$ and $(mp + nq)$ are mutually prime.

Experiment 45.

2. Suppose we select the triple $(5,12,13)$. $(13/5)^2 = 169/25$; $(13/12)^2 = 169/144$. $169/25 + 169/144 = 169/25 \times 169/144 = 28561/3600 = 7.9336111111\ldots$.

3. $c^2/a^2 + c^2/b^2 = (b^2 c^2 + a^2 c^2)/(a^2 b^2) =$

$c^2(a^2 + b^2)/(a^2 b^2) = c^2 c^2/a^2 b^2 =$

$(c/a)^2(c/b)^2$.

Experiment 46.

2. Here is one more example. Suppose we pick a = 2 and b = 9.

   Then $a^2 + b^2 = 2^2 + 9^2 = 4 + 81 = 85$.

85 = 5 x 17 and 85 = 1 x 85. Thus, we have two sets of equations.

| d - c = 5 | and | d - c = 1 |
| d + c = 17 | | d + c = 85 |

Hence c = 6, d = 11;   or   c = 42, d = 43.

Thus the two quadruples are (2,9,6,11) and (2,9,42,43).

*****

RESULTS OF EXPERIMENT GROUP 4

Experiment 47.

1.   (a) 88   (b) 888   (c) 8 888   (d) 88 888   etc.

2.   (a) 11   (b) 111   (c) 1 111   (d) 11 111 etc.

3.   1 111 111 111

4.   (a) 9   (b) 98   (c) 987   (d) 9876   (e) 98765

5.   (a) 8   (b) 188   (c) 2888   (d) 38888   (e) 488888

Experiment 48.

1.   (a) 121   (b) 12321   (c) 1 234 321   (d) 123 454 321

     (e) 12 345 654 321   (f) 1 234 567 654 321

     (g) 123 456 787 654 321   (h) 12 345 678 987 654 321

2. $1\ 111\ 111\ 111^2$ = 1 234 567 900 987 654 321

3. $111\ 111\ 111\ 111\ 111\ 111\ 111^2$ =
        12 345 679 012 345 679 012 320 987 654 320 987 654 321

Experiment 49.

1.   (a) 77   (b) 7 777   (c) 777 777   (d) 77 777 777
     (e) 7 777 777 777

2.   777 777 777 777 777 777 777 777 777 777

3.   (a) 111   (b) 1221   (c) 12321   (d) 123 321
     (e) 1 233 321   (f) 12 333 321

4.   12 333 333 333 333 333 333 333 321

98

5. (a) 63   (b) 6633   (c) 666 333   (d) 66 663 333
   (e) 6 666 633 333   (f) 666 666 333 333
   (g) 66 666 663 333 333

Experiment 50.

1. (a) 2.25   (b) 6.25   (c) 12.25   (d) 20.25   (e) 30.25
   (f) 42.25

2. (a) 1.5   (b) 2.5   (c) 3.5   (d) 4.5   (e) 5.5   (f) 6.5

3. (a) 157.5   (b) 2113.5

4. The results are 1, 3, 6, 10, 15, and 21. These are consecutive triangular numbers.

5. The square root of $n(n + 1) + .25$ is $(n + .5)$.

6. (a) 4   (b) 9   (c) 16   (d) 25   (e) 36   (f) 49

7. Each is a square.

8. 64949

9. $(n + 1)$

10. (a) 6.25   (b) 12.25   (c) 20.25   (d) 30.25   (e) 40.25
    (f) 56.25

11. Yes. They are the squares of 2.5, 3.5, 4.5, 5.5, 6.5, and 7.5.

12. 21.5

13. $(n + 1.5)^2$

15. We must add 4, the square of 2.   (a) 9   (b) 16   (c) 25
(d) 36   (e) 49   (f) 64

16. 52

17. $(n + 2)^2$

18. $[n(n + k) + (k/2)^2] = [n + (k/2)]^2$

Experiment 51.

1. (a) 25   (b) 121   (c) 361   (d) 841   (e) 1681   (f) 3025

2. Yes. They are the squares of 5, 11, 19, 29, 41, and 55. Notice that each is the product of the two middle factors minus 1. For example,

$$(3 \times 4 \times 5 \times 6) + 1 = 19^2 \quad \text{and} \quad (4 \times 5) - 1 = 19$$

3. (a) 131^2 (b) 461^2

4. $[(n + 1)(n + 2) - 1]^2$

5. (a) $121 = 11^2$ (b) $400 = 20^2$ (c) $961 = 31^2$

   (d) $1936 = 44^2$ (e) $3481 = 59^2$ (f) $5776 = 76^2$

6. (a) $[(22 \times 24) - 4]^2 = 524^2$

   (b) $[(52 \times 54) - 4]^2 = 2804^2$

7. $[(n + 2)(n + 4) - 4]^2$

8. (a) $361 = 19^2$ (b) $961 = 31^2$ (c) $2025 = 45^2$

   (d) $3721 = 61^2$ (e) $6241 = 79^2$ (f) $9801 = 99^2$

9. $3\ 876\ 961 = 1969^2$. ($1969 = 43 \times 46 - 9$.)

10. $[(n + 3)(n + 6) - 9]^2$

11. $n(n + k)(n + 2k)(n + 3k) + k^4 = [(n + k)(n + 2k) - k^2]^2$

Experiment 52.

1. (a) 3   (b) 33   (c) 333   (d) 3 333   (e) 33 333

2. 333 333 333 333

3. (a) 6   (b) 66   (c) 666   (d) 6 666   (e) 66 666

4. 666 666 666 666 666

5. (a) 23   (b) 233   (c) 2 333   (d) 23 333

6. 23 333 333 333 333 333

7. (a) 13   (b) 26   (c) 133   (d) 266   (e) 1 333   (f) 2 666

   (g) 13 333   (h) 26 666.

8. (a) 1 333 333 333 333 333   (b) 2 666 666 666 666 666

9. (a) 16   (b) 166   (c) 1 666   (d) 16 666

10. 1 666 666 666 666 666 666

12. No other single digit can appear as the repetend in such squares unless one wants to count 0, the trivial case, as in the square root of 900000000 = 30000. The only digits that can be repeated in the square roots are 3 and 6.

Experiment 53.

5. If you made no mistakes, your answer is 1089.

6. 1089

9. (a) 1089 and 9801; their digits are reversed.

   (b) 2178 and 8712   (c) 3267 and 7623   (d) 4356 and 6534

   (e) 5445, a number which is its own reverse.

10. (a) 13068 and 86031   (b) 14157 and 75141

    (c) 15246 and 64251   (d) 16335 and 53361

    (e) 25047 and 74052   (f) 26136 and 63162

    (g) 40293 and 39204. In each pair of products the digits are reversed.

12. The square roots are 33 and 99 respectively. Other such pairs include 144 and 441 (squares of 12 and 21); 10404 and 40401 (squares of 102 and 201); and 12769 and 96721 (squares of 113 and 311.)

Experiment 54

1 (a) 285714   (b) 428571   (c) 571428   (d) 714285   (e) 857142

2. 142857 x 7 = 999 999

3. (a) The sum is 27; and 2 + 7 = 9.   (b) 99   (c) 999

4. Yes. For example, 429 divided by 143 is exactly 3.

5. 588 235 294 117 647 x 17 = 9 999 999 999 999 999.

Experiment 55.

1.   If your calculator has a 10-digit display, it probably shows the square root of 123456790 to be 11111.11111 . However, if the square root of this number is carried to many places after the decimal, there are several surprising sequences of repeating digits. Here is the square root of 123456790 carried to 65 places after the decimal. The strings of repeating digits seem to get shorter and shorter the farther out we go, and finally they apparently disappear altogether.

    11 111.1111 0 555555555 41 6666666 597 222222 178819 4444
            140624 999 77213541648763

2. (a) 12345679; missing is 8.   (b) 24691358; missing is 7.

   (c) 49382716; missing is 5.   (d) 61728395; missing is 4.

   (e) 86419753; missing is 2.   (f) 98765432; missing is 1.

3. (a) 37 037 037   (b) 74 074 074   (c) 111 111 111

4. (c) 1 444 444 443   (d) 1 555 555 554   (e) 1 666 666 665

   (f) 2 333 333 331   (g) 5 888 888 883   (h) 6 888 888 882

   (i) 7 888 888 881

5. When 12345679 x 9 is multiplied by (10t + u) where (t + u) is 9 or less, the product leads off with t, followed by (t + u) repeated 8 times, followed by u.

6. (d) 4 222 222 218   (e) 4 333 333 329   (f) 5 111 111 106

   (g) 5 222 222 217   (h) 6 555 555 549   (i) 9 666 666 657

7. When 12345679 x 9 is multiplied by a whole number (10t + u) less than 90, where (t + u) is 10 or more, the product leads off with (t + 1), followed by (t + u - 9) repeated 7 times, followed by (t + u - 10), followed finally by u.